COMMU.....

Mowbray Parish Handbooks

COMMUNITY WORK

A HANDBOOK FOR
VOLUNTEER GROUPS
AND LOCAL CHURCHES

Malcolm Grundy

MOWBRAY

To George Lovell and Catherine Widdicombe,
Pioneers and enthusiasts for
Church and Community Development

Mowbray
A Cassell imprint
Villiers House
41/47 Strand
London
WC2N 5JE

387 Park Avenue South
New York
NY 10016-8810

First published 1995

British Library Cataloguing-in-Publication Data
A catalogue record for this book is available from the
British Library.

ISBN 0-264-67323-9

Typeset by York House Typographic Ltd, London
Printed and bound in Great Britain by
Biddles Ltd, Guildford and King's Lynn

Contents

HOPE

It is in the small things
That I find hope.
A meeting place for lone mothers,
A bit of advice when money is tight,
A quiet place to pour out troubles,
A listening ear when the time is right.

The days are dark, the hours are long,
Our lives are a struggle and striving,
When I lose hope,
When I feel choked
These things are lights that are lit,
Fires still burning.
Places of warmth, places of laughter.
People who are open, that you can cuddle up to.
People who are dying to know me.
Who give love, give love, give love.
And to whom it isn't returned
By us who have none to spare.
My prayer is for them
That God's love for them
Will be ecstatic.

Urban Poems, The Kairos Group

Preface

Community development work provokes extreme reactions. As I have talked to colleagues and practitioners in secular and in church situations, I am hit by two extreme moods. One is of great pessimism and suggests that a book of the kind I am preparing is like producing a manual on how to breed and keep dinosaurs just at the time when they are becoming extinct! The other mood is one of tremendous optimism. Certainly, the expectations of community work and its funding which have come to us from the 1960s and 1970s have almost completely died. No longer is there any hope of long-term or even annually repeatable funding from local authorities or major charities. The partnership which many fought to maintain between statutory and voluntary agencies have been weakened or has disappeared as financial cut-backs have decimated the old way of working.

Instead we have emerging a vibrant new world of community work, peopled by a considerably younger generation. Gone are most of the career community workers who will stay in one or a few posts for years. Gone are the ambitiously furnished projects where money was spent in the hope of solving social problems. Gone are the over-idealistic, out-of-this-world projects which were never really going to work but somehow got some money. And gone are the exclusive church projects grown in a world of ecclesiastical isolationism.

In their place are pieces of work grounded in realism and shaped through existing practice and hard work. Projects which survive are ones which have learned a sensible co-operation with other local groups and agencies. They manage their fund-raising and finances with a professionalism not previously known or needed. Workers come for a shorter term knowing that funding is likely to be for not more than three years. Training is often locally based and devised by the practitioners themselves. The

atmosphere of dependency has gone and is replaced by self-help
and inter-professional support.

Gone also is the atmosphere of rivalry about different
interpretations of community work. There are certainly different understandings of work with people and groups in the
community and I spell these out in my early chapters. The
experienced community development worker of today is a
person who will draw on different methods and interpretations
as the circumstances require.

The establishment of the Churches Community Work Alliance
(CCWA) has given a national and regional framework in which
church-related community workers can meet and develop their
own training and support systems. This network is paralleled by
the Standing Conference for Community Development and the
Federation of Community Work Training Groups, both based in
Sheffield, who provide resources and training for community
workers in more secular employment situations. Much resour-
cing is also done by the National Council for Voluntary Organizations (NCVO).

Each of these organizations produce their own publications
and broadsheets. In order to write this book I have drawn heavily
on the writings and experience of others. I am particularly
grateful to the London Voluntary Service Council for permission
to use drawings and extracts from *Just About Managing* by Sandy
Adirondack, to the William Temple Foundation for permission
to adapt material from *The New Worker*, and to Revd Dr George
Lovell for the use of his diagrams in *The Church and Community
Development*.

The poems at the end of some of the chapters come from
Despair and Hope in the City prepared by the Voice of the People
Trust. My thanks to them for their inspired work and for
permission to use the work of The Kairos Group and others.

There is so much good material available to help with
establishing new pieces of community work and with making
appointments that in one sense this book is not necessary. What I
have tried to do is to bring together the wisdom and the best from
pamphlets and booklets I have been able to discover for myself
and to focus on particular areas for this book. I hope that it will be
particularly helpful for church-related groups who are establishing a project or who are reviewing their work.

Most of the text is entirely my own and I hope that I will be
forgiven for faults and omissions. There are places where I have
used other people's writings or have tried to explain their ideas. I
hope that all acknowledgements are made and that those
mentioned will feel that I have given them a fair representation.

For the detailed 'how to' sections of the duties of officers within a project I have followed *Just About Managing* very closely indeed. I encourage readers to get this book, which offers a very comprehensive guide to the details and responsibilities of project management.

Original ideas for this book were circulated to Gill Moody, Ann Morisy, Alison Webster and Ultan Russell. I am most grateful to these people for their advice and support. The whole of the manuscript has been typed by Mrs May Farina at Avec and my thanks go to her for her considerable achievement in reading my writing. The Trustees of Avec have also been generous in allowing me the time to put together this book in a situation when we are also experiencing the pressures for survival in a difficult world. Ruth McCurry of Mowbray and I have shared ideas on community education work in east London over almost fifteen years and I thank her for the original invitation to write this book. Judith Longman took up the work of editing when she followed Ruth and my enormous gratitude goes to her for her rigour and her support.

The emerging new world of church-related community work has come about through new sources of funding from the churches. The Church Urban Fund, set up in 1984 and with more than £18 million invested, is now a major provider of funding for a very wide range of new projects. This initiative has been paralleled in the Methodist Church by the Mission Alongside the Poor Programme, though this is now merged within Methodism's considerable internal Home Missions department. In the Catholic Church the Justice and Peace Programme and the specialist social initiatives by the Catholic Bishops' Conference often have a cutting edge not known elsewhere. The move of the religious orders away from education and life in large groups into local communities living in houses of three or four has been significant in community work during the 1980s and has brought many able men and women into close identification with social issues and community problems. Also, the United Reformed Church has a long history of Community Ministers well-resourced from the centre.

In addition to these 'traditional' Christian churches, community groups and workers have now come from black-led churches and from the Asian and Afro-Caribbean communities. With these new partnerships comes the awareness of definite self-confidence, born from anger and frustration certainly, but developing with the knowledge that when communities can become empowered with a vision for their own future surprising developments will result.

Gone also is the doctrinal sense of certainty which used to accompany the pioneering stage of community work. The dramatic loss of traditional sources of funding brought first of all a defensiveness for the work and a looking back to old solutions. With the persistence of churches, old and new, in the continuing work of community development has come a new kind of worker. Many have emerged from voluntary work in local churches and have greater confidence about a public display of their faith. At the first CCWA Conference I felt I passed from being young in the church to old in community work overnight. My 1960s generation have always been unsure and even embarrassed about prayer at public conferences: perhaps a minute at the beginning, a playing of the daily news or an experimental communion service at the end was all we could manage. Here, worship was full of song and dance and music, and lasted for more than 30 minutes at the beginning of each day! This is good news for a new generation bringing confident Christian insights into renewed work.

As you move through the pages of this book I hope that we shall share our experiences, agree, disagree and learn together, and in doing so discover the God who becomes known in particular ways through the life we all share together in the building of new communities and the rebuilding of those communities which have suffered much – but survived.

MALCOLM GRUNDY

Introduction

This book will explore the many different ways in which churches can be involved in, and be enriched by their local communities. In particular there will be a guided examination of the possibilities for working with other community groups and individuals to set up a range of local projects. This work is exciting and rewarding as well as demanding and frustrating. Many of the great practical steps which need to be taken will be explored.

For those who are Christians, within churches or on the fringe, there is also an opportunity to reflect on what is happening in all this frantic activity. The God who is encountered and discovered through this work is not an external afterthought to be brought in when there is trouble or for a thanksgiving service. The God who accompanies people on their journey is the God whose presence is felt most when community is being made. Those who make the journey into community development will find themselves working with people whose values come from elsewhere and with those of other faiths. In this work of collaboration traditional ideas of God will be challenged and new experiences of spirituality will be encountered. Much unspoken love, trust, forgiveness and reconciliation will be offered and received. New horizons will be seen. The God who is with us and who goes before us will be glimpsed in new ways. When community development really works people and groups are changed, made and remade anew in ways which, when in innocence we set out on our adventures, we could never have imagined possible. If you have been there you will know; if not let me invite you, through the pages of this book, to begin your journey.

Why a book about church-related community work?

In the early discussions about this book it was thought that its contents could be general and refer to all people and groups involved in community work. As the writing developed it became clear both that the Christian churches had made an important and distinctive contribution to this work and also that there were particular questions and problems which church-related groups have to face. I use the term 'church-related' because very many pieces of work have some tenuous connection with a church rather than an existence which emerges from the life of the greater congregation. Consequently, I have written a book which is primarily for and about church groups, though all of the practical advice and information applies to any piece of community work.

It is an area of some debate as to whether the Christian churches have a distinctive and different contribution to make. At a practical and theoretical level I am sure they have. The presence of the churches in inner-city, urban and needy rural areas makes them one of the few, perhaps the only, group which has a nationwide commitment to serving and working alongside people at a very local level. The number of community work projects across the country which have, at least, some church involvement is impressive.

There is another reason for a book about church-related community work. This territory is occupied by a particular kind of idealist. Community workers and volunteers give up many human comforts, and certainly give up expectations of high wages, because they hold strong, visionary views about how society should be structured. As these chapters unfold I shall set out many of the basic criteria which will establish what community work is. I shall also go on to outline particular things, not dealt with in the general list, which Christians bring from their own values to this work. The contribution is significant and important. Values are articulated when applied to community work in ways that they are not within ordinary church life. This naming of what we are doing and why we are doing it in these particular ways needs also to be taken back into the churches for their own learning and internal development.

Christianity has always been about radical experiments in community life. From the account in the Acts of the Apostles of early Christians 'holding all things in common' we know that there were distinctive ideas about sharing and living together which believers knew was a part of their newly discovered faith. One of the most important experiments in community living comes through the experience of religious orders. Though corrupted, like all else, by human frailty, greed and the passage of time the example of Orders begun by Augustine, Benedict, Ignatius Loyola, Francis, Clare and many others speaks to us through the centuries. The Taizé Community gives ecumenical expression to that ideal today. I am surprised by how many of those involved in community work also have links with the Iona Community.

Professor Gillian Stamp from the Brunel Institute of Organisation and Social Studies, in 'The enhancement of ministry in uncertainty', says very well why the contribution of churches is essential to this, as to any other activity.

> It is the emphasis on giving meaning that is the significant insight; making it possible for people to make sufficient sense of a confused and confusing world to keep going and to help others keep going in it. While religious organizations do not have a monopoly on making meaning, they do have a long history of understanding how important it is if people are to cope and even make the most of the turbulence of their existence.

The need for definitions

Community workers tend to feel that community work is even more difficult to explain to the uninitiated than social work or teaching. They take the easy way out and describe it by reference to its concrete manifestations – lunch clubs, tenants' associations and the like. This is quite useful as it gives people a picture of what community work does, but it is not enough. Consumers need to know more. They need to know that, on the whole, professional community workers see community work as a way of working, an approach, not just as a series of end-products.

I have taken the risk of entering this minefield of definitions early on in the book. Certainly it is difficult for the outsider, and sometimes for the insider, to see the precise differences in definition among the different aspects of the work. I have also to say that to some idealistic practitioners these definitions are vital and fundamental. Work at these definitions as you read them, and where appropriate adjust your work in the light of them.

Case studies and examples

There has been some encouragement for me to illustrate the detailed parts of this book with examples of local pieces of work. I have not done this on many occasions. My reason, from the experience of my book *Light in the City*, is that stories and examples date very quickly, even when they are amalgams of 'typical' situations. Instead I have included case studies; these are in boxes in the text. In our work at Avec we have found that immersion into these situations makes them seem almost 'timeless' and allows a group member to practise by explaining another situation and to learn from their own reactions.

Most of all I hope that these chapters will come alive as their contents are matched with your own experience. If you can say 'Aha, yes, it is like that for me also', we shall have come close to building a piece of experiential community work through the dialogue of reading and of using this book.

1

Churches and
Communities

Community development work is about life in a two-way street. If the idea of developing people and communities is to have any meaning at all it has to have a basis in communication between people and groups. One-way streets mean that traffic follows nose to tail. Motorways are fast but are also one-way streets. It might be possible to travel from one place to another very quickly but it is done at the expense of meeting people on the way who are travelling in different directions and who have different experiences and stories to tell. Fast travel hardly gives time to speak to those who are going in your own direction.

The involvement of local and national churches in building up community life has to include a two-way dialogue. It is vital that there should be an exchange of ideas and a listening to the experiences of people and groups who have different beliefs and practices from their own. Churches, and the Christians who make up them, are part of a community. Indeed, local communities are the raw material from which church life is drawn. It might be best at the beginning of this book, then, to emphasize what communities give to the churches before attention is given in much greater detail to what churches can give to communities.

Communities are not raw material, fodder, for churches to use to undertake their work and projects. Communities and churches are partners in which each gives to the other in a reciprocal relationship. It is in the life and discoveries flowing from that relationship that the God who works in community is experienced.

What communities give to churches

Communities first of all give people! The enormous varieties of need in any society emerge because people live together in communities. They have a rich range of talents and expertise.

People have skills and money which they contribute to the life of their local area. Some people have time and ability to devote to the needs of their area. They will join in running drama groups, parents' groups for schools, bowls, tennis, cricket and football clubs, and many other local activities in which groups contribute to the variety of local community life.

Some people will be more aware of local need and will want to form or join groups which either provide help or lobby for improvements. Local people offer to their communities time to organize clubs for old people, drop-in centres, residents' groups and much more. Many of their activities make demands on churches to participate in the life of a local community, and of course, many local activities and organizations will contain church members.

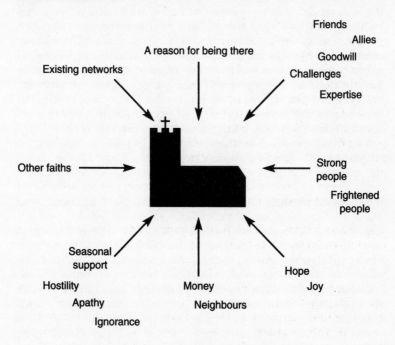

What communities give to the churches

Communities give much to churches in an external way. Primarily they produce the wealth, in a whole range of ways, which enables money to be given to churches and church activities as well as to local voluntary organizations. Very many church buildings came into existence through the generosity of some local business. East Anglia has many 'wool churches' built when the medieval wool trade was at its height. Many industrial towns have a 'railway church' built by one of the private railway companies for communities of workers. Each region and locality will have its own examples.

Today wealth comes to churches, especially for community work, through local and central government grants as well as through private giving. English Heritage helps fortunate and architecturally distinguished churches with repairs. Local authorities, in a whole range of ways, help with grants for the provision of welfare services. We certainly lament the severely reduced amounts of money from these sources but on a national scale they are still considerable.

More than anything else neighbourhoods provide the context in which churches operate. Most churches take their characteristics from the type of community in which they are set. Needs to which churches can respond are local needs – unemployment, poverty, poor housing, single-parent families, drug abuse, racial disharmony – as well as national issues, and these provide churches with the context within which they work. Communities also provide the constituency from which members will be drawn. Church members, much as they often might look and feel it, are not people from another planet. They come from largely the same area as those they are working alongside. They share the same hopes, needs and frustrations as everyone else.

What churches offer to their communities

Churches offer more to their communities than they are aware. I owe it to colleagues in Germany and Scandinavia for pointing out what expertise we have for mobilizing voluntary effort. Many colleagues in countries where churches are funded by a local state tax have said that appeals in their churches for voluntary help would largely fall upon deaf ears. The reply would be: 'We pay someone to do that, why are you asking us to give up our free time?' British churches, however, have a tradition going right back to their foundations of voluntary involvement in education, health care and welfare work within local communities. Today this takes on a somewhat different appearance but the tradition and the expertise remain to a much greater extent than we are often aware.

The greatest practical resource which churches offer to the community is their local nature. Overlain on top of one another, local churches cover our countries with a network of very local organizations. With local churches, now in a wide variety of ways, go local ministries. While not primarily community workers, and not trained as such, local priests and ministers often have a much wider commitment to working in a community than the limits of their local church might suggest. They are there through the week and can offer themselves for committee and practical work when many others are not available.

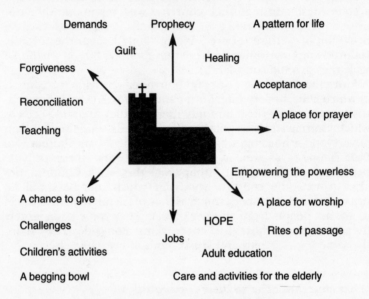

Demands   Prophecy   A pattern for life

Guilt   Healing

Forgiveness   Acceptance

Reconciliation   A place for prayer

Teaching

Empowering the powerless

A chance to give   A place for worship

Challenges   HOPE   Rites of passage

Jobs

Children's activities   Adult education

A begging bowl   Care and activities for the elderly

What churches give to their communities

Why do you want to get involved?

Before you decide to go ahead and get involved in a community project of any kind consider changing your mind. Very many people who get caught up in stressful, expensive and time-consuming community projects wish that they had never begun. Consider the possibility that you may be mistaken, that the need does not really exist, or that you are not the person or the group best equipped to meet it. Often frustration emerges with a piece of work because it was begun without a proper assessment of a situation or with motives which, even if unexpressed, were more to do with self-interest and self-fulfilment than with a genuine meeting of the needs of others in a community.

Service or evangelism?

It may well be that no discussion ever takes place about the way in which a piece of community work will increase the size of a congregation. For many people this is a conversation which does not need to take place because 'evangelism' leading to church-going is never a part of their motive for doing any piece of social service. Often, and unfortunately, projects are established quite independently of the life of regular church-goers and the two never meet. For many other Christians 'virtue is its own reward' and a lifetime of disinterested service characterizes their Christian witness. Many projects will be done in partnership with other groups, each with their own reason or motive for involvement. However, when a project drains energy or uses time which might otherwise be given to more obviously 'church' events then a tension might arise. Struggling churches may see a lively project in their hall or crypt as a lifeline which could increase their numbers. Churches who have a high emphasis on the need to share their faith may well experience a tension when nothing overtly 'Christian' is seen to be taking place.

Communication is a vital factor. Possibilities for misunderstanding and disaster are great if a project is seen as the minister's particular interest which is taking him or her away from traditional expectations of the role as pastor, service taker and administrator. An active group managing a project, with non-churchgoers brought in, can be seen as a powerful group within a local church. They will probably be handling larger sums of money than the Church Council and may well be employing staff. The question of whether workers in church community projects should be 'Christians' is often an area for debate and dispute.

There are many ways in which evangelism can be done. A recent report for the Decade of Evangelism has concluded that the majority of people in churches have come to their faith gradually, often with support from a few personal friends. Others are impressed by the example of Christians and churches and feel attracted by what they see. Moments of conversion and decisions following a particular piece of preaching or a rally are understood as stages in a journey towards deeper commitment.

Community work, and community service, fit very well into this pattern. Visiting the elderly, providing a drop-in centre, creating work for those who are unemployed, setting up a mother and toddler group with young mums, and the like are all pieces of work which are done for their own sake. A need is recognized and a group of people in the community get together

and offer help. It would, in fact, be a surprise in many places if
the churches were not involved as partners in such work. Motives
are very transparent. Children, teenagers, the disabled, the
elderly or any group which is 'being helped' soon see through the
pretence if other motives than those of a desire to help are
present. Genuine values and deeply held beliefs become apparent gradually, over quite a long period of time, as relationships
become established and experiences are shared together. The
story of Jesus walking with the disciples on the Emmaus Road is
always an impressive one (Luke 24.13–35). It is in the shared
journeys and in telling stories of life's experiences to one another
than the Lord is discovered and is found to be walking with his
people.

Congregations who are hoping for some form of evangelistic
success will have to be aware of the consequences should they
succeed. New and often quite different people will start coming
to church. If they have come through involvement in a 'successful' community project they may well be used to joining in
discussion group activity. They will probably be used to decisions
being made in a participative way and they will want to join in
discussions about liturgy, music, the ordering of the church and
the like. They may also come into congregational life through a
working relationship with the vicar which will be different from
the more respectful 'traditional' approach of many in the
congregation. All these adjustments are the possible consequences of evangelism as a result of community work. Church
growth is positive and dynamic, it is also radical and a disturber of
old practices. Its consequences need to be recognized and
prepared for when churches and community development come
close together.

CASE STUDY
A community hall for the parish

Three years ago I had just arrived as a curate in my first
parish and was very anxious to begin anything in community work. My first meeting was with a group of middle-
aged women and a few men who wanted to renovate an old
church school as a community hall. Without bothering to
check on the wisdom of this proposal I threw myself into the
project.

A meeting was called of people from all over the parish
but only those living closest to the school showed any real
interest. At the same time the parish priest stated that he

was willing for use to be made of the school provided that it was used for the benefit of the whole parish. I invited a few people from outside the parish, but living close to the school, to become involved. Very quickly a new group formed, only half of whom are parishioners.

They have worked very hard for three years to complete the renovation of the building. However they have alienated a number of younger people who attempted to work with them. To satisfy the parish priest they have invited people from other areas of church life to help with fundraising, but with little response.

Since the project began we have defined our purpose in the parish: to see in five years' time a just and worshipping Christian community.

The present situation is: quite a few of the people in the project are not church members; many in the congregation do not seem to be interested in the project, at least at this difficult stage; and the condition still stands that the centre is for the whole parish.

I would like to see the committee being more open to newcomers and especially young people. I am also concerned that the building committee should take responsibility for planning activities after the Centre opens. (Or should I simply allow things to float and see who is attracted to use the building?) One other thing, a monthly collection is taken in pubs and clubs outside the church. I feel some responsibility to make sure that those who contribute and wish to use the Centre have opportunities to do so.

What action should I take next?

Preparing the ground

Many community projects and pieces of work come from small beginnings. They frequently grow without even those involved being aware of the scale of what they are taking on, or what its consequences might be. Reports to the Church Council, an appropriate church management group, trustees, stewards, deacons or whatever are vital. The more people feel that they are consulted and involved, if only at a distance, the more they are likely to support the work. This is equally the case in making reports to local ecumenical groups: 'Churches Together' as Councils of Churches are now often called. Reporting can bring in allies and resources and often prevent individual churches competing with similar pieces of work. They can be a great asset in providing accurate information about the nature of a local community.

A local audit or survey

Frequently, churches and church groups have unrealistic expectations of the kind of outreach which is needed or which is possible in their area. The way to establish whether there really are 'lots of lonely old people out there' or 'legions of lonely single parents trapped in their homes with young children' is to undertake a survey. The term 'audit' has become a popular way to describe this work. Very many organizations have produced audit packs for local churches and groups to use. They vary in emphasis according to the work which needs to be done and the resources which a local church may have. Rural areas may have one set of concerns while urban or industrial areas may have a different emphasis.

One thing is absolutely certain: an audit will begin to get a church engaged with its local population, other community groups and its local authority. The very act of going out and listening and asking questions will gain allies. The church will be seen to be taking an interest in its locality. For the first time, some people will come to see the relevance of Christianity in their lives. The experience of many local churches is that through the survey new friends were made and more effective resources became available to begin to construct a project.

If churches do not consult then it cannot be said that they are engaging in community development. They may be providing services *for* people but they are not working *with* them. A shared piece of community development work will arise from those who have needs in a community working together and with local groups and agencies for the strengthening of local human and material resources.

One example of a local audit

Adapted from the audit outlined in *Faith in the City*.

Why do it?

The audit should be used to help the local church to understand itself in its situation, to reflect on its purpose, and then to make plans for becoming a more effective, outward-looking and participating church.

How to do it?

This will vary from church to church.

(a) The Church Council should come to a common mind as to whether it is prepared for an audit. If it is, it should ask a small group to organize the audit. The group should:

- be as representative of the congregation as possible (by age, sex, length of membership, etc.)
- include one or two 'outsiders' sympathetic to the church and representative of the locality
- involve an outside consultant from the deanery or diocese to advise in setting up the audit and discussing the results.

(b) It should involve the congregation and community and be done as simply and imaginatively as possible.
(c) It should be completed within six months to a year.

The audit

The audit has two parts: the analysis of the locality and the church, and planning for action.

Part 1: The analysis of the locality and the church

The locality

The aim of this analysis is to build an accurate picture of the parish.

The map A large map of the neighbourhood should be made showing:

- its boundary and neighbouring churches; the church and other buildings
- major roads
- bus routes
- major meeting places – for example, sub-post offices, super-markets, shops, schools, social and community centres, pubs, fish and chip shops, off-licences, newsagents (all with appropriate symbols using differently coloured gummed stars)
- hospitals, old people's homes, etc.
- housing – with blocks coloured differently for council, private rented, owner-occupied; high-rises and demolition areas should also be marked.

The people A separate statistical profile should be prepared to accompany the map. This profile can be built up with information from the 1991 Census and from other sources. Local authorities can be of particular help here. It should include a population estimate and a breakdown of the parish or area by:

- age
- sex
- employment
- ethnic groups
- mobility (how long on average do people live in the parish?)

Suggestion as to how to do this analysis can be found in:
Towards Local Social Analysis, Church Urban Action on Poverty, 27 Blackfriars Road, Salford M3 7AQ.
Discovering the Poor: A kit for local groups, Urban Theology Unit, 210 Abbeyfield Road, Sheffield S4 7AZ
Mission Audit, Board of Mission and Unity, CIO Publishing, Church House, Great Smith Street, London SW1P 3NZ.

What do people feel about the area? One way to do this is to ask people to write down the ten things they dislike about the area, and the ten things they enjoy or value about it ('ten for sorrow, ten for joy') in a brainstorming session. It is helpful to get the view of different groups – youth club, OAPs, young parents, etc.; it is also important to get the views of people and groups outside the congregation. The results should be analysed.
Are there conflicts in the area? (Young/old, newcomers/established residents, middle class/working class, etc.)

The church

The aim of this profile is to begin to build an accurate picture of the local church. A simple questionnaire, completed by all members over a period of a month, is the quickest way to get information about the people. It should be brief enough to be completed after the service without difficulties. The results need careful analysis. Suggested questions are:

- employment status (waged, unwaged, retired, part-time, full-time, etc.)
- class: what is or has been your job (or your spouse's)?
- age (or age-group)
- length of church membership
- do you live in or out of the parish? If the latter, are you within one mile or further away?
- which service(s) do you come to, and how often?

- what kind of housing do you live in? (owner-occupied, council rented, private rented, etc.)
- what are your skills or hobbies?

Those undertaking the audit should also, as a group, seek answers to the following questions about the church:

- church membership: numbers and distribution in relation to the map, types of housing, etc.
- usual Sunday attendance, and trends in recent years
- who are the key people/leaders, and why?
- what proportion of the congregation is handicapped?
- what activities does the church run, and why?
- what activities are the church and its individual members involved in in the community?
- premises: what are they, in what condition are they, who uses them and when? Is the church left open during the week?
- financial trends (budget five years ago and last year, and the likely budget in the coming year)
- how much does the congregation give to the church per head per week?

Part 2: Planning for action

The aim of planning for action is to help the congregation to come to conclusions about the nature of the parish and the congregation, and to see the need for the church to make certain changes in its life and practice if it is to be properly local and outward-looking. This planning needs to be done carefully and over a period of time (certainly several months), maybe using particular groups, but always involving the whole congregation in the final decisions.

It may be useful to use four stages in this planning:

1. The audit group should put together in a simple and imaginative way all the evidence from the analysis of the locality and church, and present it to the congregation. A visual display is particularly important. Discussion should only aim to clarify and agree the emerging picture of parish and church.
2. Questions now need to be asked of the church to discover how effective it is as a church. These questions could include:
   (a) Are local people and cultures, including members of minority ethnic groups, represented

- in the congregation?
- in the worship?

- in church leadership?
- among church officials, sidespeople, leaders of parish organizations?
- on the Church Council?
- on deanery or other wider groups?
- on regional boards, councils and committees, and synods?

(b) Is the church seeking to be present in the various neighbourhoods, organizations and institutions in the parish:

- in the location of its worship centres?
- in social outreach projects – including caring schemes, youth work, unemployment projects, etc.?
- in house groups?
- through chaplaincies?
- are there parts of the local area unrepresented in the church?

(c) Do the church buildings (church, hall, centre, school, etc.) and their use reflect a church which is properly local and outward-looking? For example:

- are they used for and by local people and cultures, including other religions?
- are they used as drop-in centres for the unemployed, or as advice centres?
- are there obstacles to such aims, and if so how can they be removed?
- can church land be used for community purposes?

(d) Is the church served by a team of ministries including

- clergy and deacons?
- lay ministries?
- senior church officers (wardens, etc.)?
- to what extent is ministry shared between clergy and laity?

(e) Is the church collaborating fully

- with other denominations?
- with other parishes?
- with the denominational boards and councils?
- with other local organizations, local authorities, etc.?

(f) Is the church actively involved in training its members for such ministries and mission? What kind of training would be most helpful?

(g) Are there any needs in the area (or of neighbouring parishes) which could be met in whole or part through the skills or hobbies of church members?

(h) Is there anything that can be done in collaboration with other faiths?

3. In answering these questions, particular objectives for a church concerned to be more effective in an Urban Priority Area (UPA) will begin to emerge. These provisional objectives should be illuminated by a study of the Christian tradition, especially the Bible. Questions to be asked could include: Have the people of God faced this or similar situations before, and what was their response? Are there contemporary examples of similar situations being faced by other congregations, and what solutions have they tried? Are there any diocesan specialists, or others, who can help us?

4. This should lead to a congregation deciding on its objectives, and selecting several priorities for the first year. These should include concrete projects. Projects and other objectives should not be attempted on every front in the first year. Changes should be accomplished gradually over a period of years with careful monitoring and discussion.
Inevitably deep questions will arise about the nature and purpose of the church and the meaning of the Christian Gospel. People should be encouraged to face them, even if there is a disagreement, as long as the discussion leads to action and is not an evasion of it. A sufficient common mind is needed simply for the next step.

Although perhaps reluctant to admit it, the local church offers a vision for society. This is done in a wide variety of ways. Christians do believe we are all equal in the sight of God and it follows that, in their own quiet and local ways, many church people will be working to see wrongs put right. Very few will be open political activists and would be embarrassed if they were told they were working for social justice. Nevertheless their influence through a vision of society is considerable.

Very many more people will be moved to help through the inspiration of the parables of Jesus. The Good Samaritan, who gave time and resources to help a person who had been attacked by robbers, still inspires many and has a contemporary ring. It was the story of Dives and Lazarus, of the gap between the rich and the needs of the poor, which inspired Albert Schweitzer to begin his medical work in Africa. As Christians think more about these activities many are drawn to the Old Testament to see how God works through people. Spiritual progress and a right relationship with God become understood as a community as well as a personal activity.

Much will be made elsewhere in this book of the physical resources which churches can offer to their communities. Church buildings and halls ripe for adaptation provide places where people can meet, and offer potential premises for all kinds of projects. The local church is a great community resource, with its feet placed firmly on the ground.

Further Reading

Faith in the City (Church House Publishing, 1985)
Living Faith in the City (General Synod of the Church of England, 1990)
Theology in the City, Anthony Harvey (ed.) (SPCK, 1989)
Faith in the Countryside (Churchman Publishing, 1990)
Rural Anglicanism, Leslie Francis (Collins, 1985)
Faith in Leeds (Leeds Church Community Involvement Project, c/o Salem United Reformed Church, 43 Hunslet Road, Leeds LS10 1JW)
Let's Do Theology, Laurie Green (Mowbray, 1990)
Despair and Hope in the City, Philip and Jonathan Evans (Voice of the People Trust, c/o 277 Reddings Lane, Tyseley, Birmingham B11 3DD)

2

What is Community Work?

Churches are involved in community work in a variety of ways. Church members as individuals help their neighbours out by doing shopping or other errands, by getting prescriptions or by keeping a garden tidy. Clergy frequently get asked to sit on local committees as a representative of their church or of the churches in their area. Some clergy find themselves involved in the life of a local school. Many are deeply involved in church schools, often as Chair of the Governors. There are many churches who hold jumble sales, ostensibly to raise money for themselves or for a good cause. However they are also providing a source of cheap clothing and other bric-à-brac for the not-so-well-off. Flower festivals and concerts in church make a cultural or aesthetic contribution to community life.

There are many who will say that the very presence of a dignified, well-kept church in an area is a symbol for community memories of many kinds. A church building can give a 'heart' to a community which might otherwise appear to be little more than rows of houses with the occasional pub or shop.

All these things are contributions to community life but they are not community work as such. There are many ways in which community work can be described and understood. There is no doubt that definitions overlap, with no one method of working claiming clear territory all of its own, and the different methods of working are not without controversy among the practitioners themselves. It may be helpful to describe these methods of working so that those who have become involved in some form of community activity or other can understand and analyse their work. Definitions are also a great help as reference points when work is being reviewed and evaluated. We are encouraged to stand back from the compulsive activity of community work to ask what it actually is.

Community care

The emphasis in this kind of activity is in mobilizing volunteers and groups in a community so that resources are offered more effectively to other people. The emphasis is on doing things *for* other people. Neighbourhood care schemes aim to bring people together and to bring about caring relationships.

It is worth exploring motives for being involved in neighbourhood care. For some the motivation will be fairly basic: 'I like helping people', 'I know some people in need, and I want to get something going . . .'. But others will have different motives. For example, a community worker employed by the Social Services department may have a 'brief' for developing neighbourhood care. The community worker's reason for 'bringing people together' may be very different from that of the local residents. This is why the ownership of the work must be discussed at length in the early stages of a scheme. The needs and resources of the neighbourhood are likely to be varied. Who decides the needs affects the way local people see their role and determine their level of involvement. If you work for an agency, you cannot impose your ideas and preconceptions on a developing scheme if you wish to secure the commitment of others.

There are basically two approaches to the setting up of neighbourhood care schemes. One approach is to use the 'volunteer' model; the other is to use the 'community development' model. In most schemes the approaches overlap but the emphasis of a scheme – whether on volunteers or the community – is important because of the way it is perceived by those involved and by those in the community.

The volunteer method

To look at the volunteer method of organization it is helpful to use a real example. Greystone Good Neighbours is a scheme operating in a north London borough which was studied by the Neighbourhood Care Action Programme in 1983. (See *Neighbourhood Care in Practice*, Rodney Hedley (LVSC, 1984).)

The aim of Greystone Good Neighbours in its own words is: 'To link men and women of goodwill who are able to help their neighbours, with those who need that help. If you live in Greystone you may sometimes find yourself a helper, and sometimes being helped.' Volunteer helpers are recruited; they join the scheme by stating the sorts of help they are prepared to give, and when they are available. The Greystone Good Neighbours publicity leaflet serves as a registration form and has a 'prompt' list of tasks:

Can you

- cook meals, provide meals?
- give domestic help?
- look after children?
- take children to school?
- babysit?
- do shopping?
- provide transport?
- give out GGN publicity?
- visit people?
- do odd jobs?
- sit in with frail adults?
- read to people?
- write letters?
- help generally?
- be a local contact?

Volunteers are then called upon when there is a request for help. Requests come to Greystone Good Neighbours from people (clients) themselves, or through request agents, such as social workers, district nurses or home helps. The person requiring help is matched up – usually by task and geography – to the person offering it. The scheme relies heavily on the organizational abilities of the co-ordinator.

Another element of Greystone Good Neighbours is the local contact system. Here the intention is to decentralize the scheme. People offering themselves as local contacts attempt to recruit people or make sure they know of a number of people in their own street or road and ask them for help when the need arises. Local contacts also seek out those who may need help. They do this by displaying a 'Good Neighbour' plate on their house front. In one sense the local contact system is a less formal version of the Good Neighbour scheme itself.

Most volunteer schemes reach the stage where they decide to draw up a formal constitution and have a Management Committee. The way Greystone Good Neighbours is governed is shown in the diagram below. The Greystone Council of Churches, which originally sponsored the scheme, is still very much in evidence. The committee is meant to overview the work. In the case of volunteer schemes the 'co-ordinator' in the office is the one most 'overviewed'. Volunteer helpers and clients usually air their views at Annual General Meetings or, if the scheme organizes them, at 'get togethers' like coffee mornings.

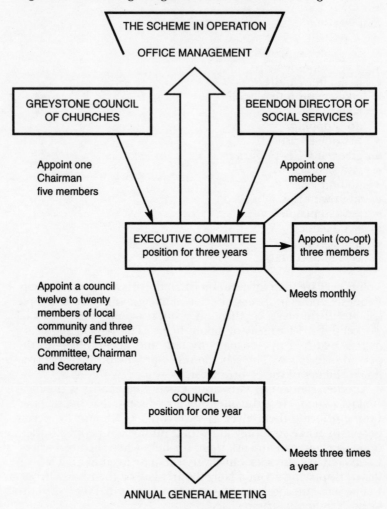

Governing structure of Greystone Good Neighbours

Advantages

- people volunteering can be precise about what they are offering
- people asking for help can be precise about their needs

- evaluation of the scheme is easier: jobs are done, or are not done
- many valuable one-to-one relationships can be formed
- the scheme can make its brief clear to other helping agencies
- especially useful for those who are housebound.

Disadvantages

- people volunteering and accepting help can feel very isolated. With all work channelled through a co-ordinator, participants are not aware of the range of resources available
- the scheme can be abused by agencies keen to get the 'job done' at any cost
- people may feel shy about expressing their needs
- much of the responsibility for the scheme is left in the hands of a few individuals. They may become distant from the neighbourhood and the scheme's participants.

There are many variants on the volunteer model described at Greystone. Some schemes:

- make no attempt to devolve their operation, having a centralized system perhaps covering a whole borough
- are a loose coalition or federation of small area/street-based groups working on the local contact basis
- will not accept requests directly from the public
- have a specific worker to vet volunteers (written references may have to be obtained before a volunteer can be accepted)
- issue cards to all the households in the neighbourhood for display for anyone to use in time of need.

Whatever the variant, the emphasis of volunteer schemes is to give service or help to others. Volunteer Bureaux in towns all over Britain are doing excellent work by co-ordinating volunteers and local needs in this way. (Much of the material for this section has been adapted from *Your Neighbourhood Group*, published by the Neighbourhood Care Action Programme in 1985.)

Community work

Community work differs from 'Volunteering' in that it tries to gain the active involvement of individuals and groups within a community. It attempts to mobilize action on local issues in order to bring about improvements. Attempts are made to focus on issues which affect the lives of people within a community and to mobilize people and resources in such a way that improvements can be gained by mutual co-operation and common action.

Community workers and community groups have spent much time in recent years trying to find an agreed definition of community work. The following definition was arrived at through a process of consultation between black and white, male and female community workers instigated by the Federation of Community Work Training Groups in 1989:

Community work is about the active involvement of all people in the issues which affect their lives.

Firstly, it is about the ability of all people to act together to create environments where they can reflect and act on their collective concerns to challenge inequalities and influence and assert control over social, economic and political issues. Community work aims to change the balance of power which will facilitate local democracy. In this sense community work focuses on relations between people and those institutions (both public and private) which shape their everyday lives.

Secondly, community work is about acknowledging the specific experience and contribution of black people and women, whilst involving the experience and developing the skills and knowledge of all people to take collective action for change.

Thirdly, community work must take a lead in confronting the attitudes and behaviour of individuals and institutions which discriminate against all powerless groups. Community work is a process which encourages participatory democracy. This process focuses on a wide range of issues affecting the poor and disadvantaged. These include employment, housing, health, finance, work with young people, etc. But whatever the issues the work will always combine the above three elements.

In practice, community work enables workers in the community to:

- recognize the values with which they work
- gain strength from collective action
- develop confidence, knowledge and skills
- develop an awareness and understanding of the issues and the structural causes of social problems
- become empowered to create new, more equal relationships between the consumer and providers of service
- establish new forms of association
- take action to confront, challenge and break down prejudice.

Many agencies now take the above approach to community work as their starting point, these include:

- the Association of Metropolitan Authorities

- the Standing Conference for Community Development
- the Care Sector Consortium – Voluntary Organizations Group (Community Work)
- the Federation of Community Work Training Groups
- the Association of Community Workers
- the Churches Community Work Alliance.

The actual emphasis of the above definition focuses on empowerment. It asks who the people who experience power-lessness in Britain are and comes close to defining the constituency whom community work needs to involve.

Included in the term 'community worker' is anyone who is actively involved in the ideas expressed within the definition. It excludes those workers whose community tag is because they are simply out-posted in the community. It excludes those professionals who are extending their social or policing functions into the community on the terms of their own agency, not the community they serve. A policy of community care, for example, which simply seeks to co-opt the efforts of local people without also looking at issues of local control and accountability, does not fall within the ambit of community work as we have described it.

Values and theology

Those with a religious belief will almost certainly want to add their own values to any definition of community work. Values arise from a personal faith and an understanding of the scriptures:

- a vision of a co-operative society in which people live together peacefully and control the environment in which they live
- a perspective on humanity that gives equal value to all people whatever their condition. This leads to a positive attempt to confront attitudes and practices that discriminate against disadvantaged groups, especially black people and women
- a view of equality and justice that acknowledges the right of all people to have equal chances of meeting human needs for income, housing, education, health and a safe environment
- a commitment to sharing power and responsibility with people in the community. This need not to be the place where people live, but can be a community of interest, such as the local church congregation
- a recognition that genuine participation and collaborative styles of work are to the benefit of all who are involved and are the most creative ways of solving problems.

It is important to reflect on the connections between those values and the central themes in scripture and the Christian tradition. The theological basis for church engagement in community work draws on several strands of belief. One strand is the vision of a Kingdom of God, where all live in community and where there is real interdependence and interrelatedness. Another is the search and struggle for justice and righteousness contained in many of the most powerful biblical stories. God calls men and women to change systems and structures that diminish people and leave them powerless. A third strand is the preciousness and uniqueness of each person, created in the image of God but also only able to be fully human when in relationship to others. Fourth, there is in many of the gospel stories an attentiveness to experience. Again and again Jesus found a way of relating to people that took their experience seriously – whether of poverty, wealth, bereavement or sickness. He started where they were and acknowledged their own needs and fears.

The process and the participatory method

If these values are to be maintained, then the way in which the work is undertaken becomes the most important factor. The methods used will need to reinforce the process. This method is one which involves action and reflection. It starts with action. A group will come together and reflect on what has happened so far, then plan the strategy and go out and do it better next time.

Every group is made up of individuals, all of whom experience action in a different way. A white person's perspective will not be the same as that of a black person, an able-bodied person's not the same as a differently abled person, a woman's not the same as a man's. People also learn in different ways. Knowledge and expertise are built up gradually through a range of different experiences. Most people gain understanding by hanging new learning on hooks of previous learning. For some people, learning is blocked because their particular experience is never part of the learning. Unless the experiences of black people, of women, of other powerless groups in society are incorporated, valued and confirmed, some people will continue to be marginalized.

Powerlessness is both a personal and a political issue, and community work has the responsibility for linking the personal learning which empowers individuals to the collective learning which empowers communities. Because of this, understanding power and powerlessness within society is essential learning for community workers. It is the process of action and reflection that brings this home.

Methods need to take account of the experience people bring with them. This means learning *not* to separate the personal from the political, otherwise personal liberation will not take place through collective action. If individuals are marginalized the action will be of marginal value.

The Ten Commandments of community work

From a definition of community work and a description of the values which underpin it can come principles which form almost a 'check-list' for good community work practice. They can also be defined negatively – if at least some of these principles are not present then the activity, however worthy, cannot be described as community work.

1. Respect of human rights
2. Vision of a society which is truly a participatory democracy, and where people contribute and receive as equals
3. Recognition that collaborative and collective working within our democracy is not always by equals, and that there are inequalities within communities which are severely damaged
4. Belief in the ability of all people to work positively together to change inequality
5. That community work must involve a process of action and reflection which moves towards clear goals, set collectively and evaluated continually
6. That such a process must also enable the empowerment of those with the least power, so that they can participate as equals
7. That groups must be self-determining, with those experiencing the problem in control of the outcomes
8. That individuals take responsibility for themselves and their own actions, and then recognize the influence their values have on other people. These values must constantly be appraised in the light of new learning
9. Giving support to individuals, groups and communities so that they can deal with conflict, and can challenge for themselves inequality and injustice
10. Appreciation of each other and the reality of each other's experience, and confirming and validating this as part of a process for real change within society.

Community development

It may seem like splitting hairs to distinguish between community work and community development. There is certainly some controversy in trying to distinguish between the two. Some of the differences are of background and history as people and groups have influenced the debate. More than anyone else T. R. Batten has given an emphasis to the 'development' aspects of community work. His experience was in West Africa and as a lecturer providing courses for students from developing countries at London University. Revd Dr George Lovell, a Methodist minister in Croydon and founder of Avec, studied with him and has been one of the principal promoters of community development ideas in Britain and Ireland through the 1970s and 1980s. They would set out their understanding of community development in the following ways.

Community development is concerned with helping people of all ages to grow and mature *by and through* assisting them to decide, plan and take action to improve their physical environment and social amenities. It is about what ordinary people in local situations can do to improve their lives and what happens to them as they do this.

The primary emphasis in a community development project is not what people do for themselves or for others, but the effect on all those involved by their participation in the activity. In a community development project changes in people are more important than changes in physical amenities. The ways in which change takes place, and an understanding of them, are more significant in the long term than the immediate material gain.

Those involved in community development try to help build communities by working *with* people rather than *for* them. We might say, to give an example, that people work *for* bosses or employers, customers or clients; they work *with* friends and colleagues.

A Christian perspective

Church-based community development work will increasingly mean that churches do not 'go it alone' but will work with Christians from other denominations and with people outside church life. They will be regarded as equals in the work because of what unites them in their commitment to the project or the cause. They will be united in activity for an agreed end but the beliefs underlying their activity may be quite different.

Christians will need to be clear about their own beliefs and motives. Our beliefs may stem from our understanding of God as Creator. But God works in and through people too. Community development work works *with* people to continue the processes of creation and of stewardship.

We may also have an understanding of our beliefs leading to action in a 'servant ministry'. Traditionally in many very good pieces of work through the centuries this has been seen as doing things *for* other people. In contrast, the servant ministry of Jesus was not of this kind. He was a servant to all, and his actions showed this. His methods demonstrated that he worked *with* people, he gave them choices and opportunities. Their development took place as they worked with Jesus on the things which concerned them. He was appropriately called 'Emanuel' which means 'God with us'.

Christian community work which emphasizes the changes which take place in people when we work *with* them rather than *for* them is activity which demonstrates a God-like and a Christ-like activity. It builds a sense of community based on a partnership of equals, where the words 'we' and 'our' are more important than the words 'them' and 'us'.

In his book *The Church and Community Development*, George Lovell has a diagram showing the effectiveness of two different kinds of work of community building on a new housing estate. Scheme A has church people visiting individuals who are lonely. Scheme B has far fewer people visiting but their method is to involve many others and thus create a more effective, and lasting, pattern of supportive relationships. People in the community became involved as well as church members.

Community development goes on from this local, one-church piece of activity to involve other churches and form alliances with other organizations. In this way development takes place across a much wider community. Greater strength can command greater resources and gain more lobbying power. Churches and community groups are able to employ workers to work with them in furthering their aims.

Advantages

- people are not labelled 'clients' or 'volunteers'
- the network can be more natural, as people choose those they want to be involved with
- the group can form an identity and address itself to common needs, e.g. transport, housing, etc. The scheme can become political with a small 'p'.

Disadvantages

- evaluation is difficult – people are never quite sure whether needs are being met/jobs are being done

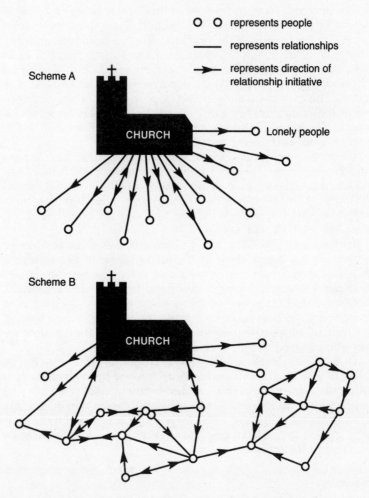

Visiting lonely people on a new housing estate

- the group may become 'clique-like' – new people find it hard to become involved
- more resources may be needed for the group – premises for meetings, for example
- management may be difficult – a committee may be 'in charge' but the everyday mix of people expressing their views may cause conflict
- communication may be difficult because of the numbers of people involved; there may be confusion about roles.

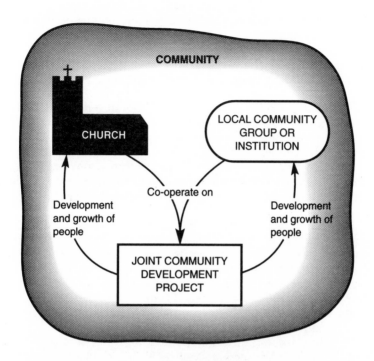

Community development
Reproduced with permission from *The Church and Community Development*

Community development is often described as 'the long way round'. Certainly working in this way does, initially, take longer. It requires a strong sense of vision and commitment. Patience is a virtue and in the initial stages of consultation and waiting for others, frustration and failure may be more apparent than quick results and success. It is in the longer term when stability, continuity and changed relationships are experienced that the value of this method of working can be fully appreciated.

Community organizing or broad-based organizing

For many people the slow, local, participative methods of most community work do not act quickly, or publicly, enough to address serious situations. They will argue that a much sharper, high-profile activity is needed. Some problems – those of bad housing conditions, of racial inequality, of inadequate policing or social service provision – require political solutions. Resources will only be released if a very public debate takes place with political lobbying and press coverage.

The American Saul Alinsky is the person most associated with
the development of this kind of political community activity.
Alinsky worked in Chicago during the 1940s and 1950s. At first
he worked with scattered, voiceless groups, mobilizing them to
protest about their living and working conditions. An interviewer
in *Playboy* magazine described him as 'a community organizer
who looks like an accountant and talks like a stevedore'. His main
base of activity became the Industrial Areas Foundation (IAF)
where he trained community organizers to work in many other
cities of the United States.

Alinsky's method of working is called community organizing
and involves the mobilizing of community groups and agencies
for local political action in furtherance of their grievances. The
term now preferred is 'broad-based organizing'.

The aim of broad-based organizing is the empowerment of
people who may normally be passive subjects of others who are in
positions of influence or power. It gives the powerless a voice in
decision-making. It is based on the presumption that local people
are the best judge of what they need; and the principle of never
doing for others what they can do for themselves, but instead
equipping them to play an active part in determining their own
lives, is paramount.

This type of organizing's methodology has a number of
features. First it is *'broad-based'* – it is an organization of
organizations with a diverse membership. Groups join as community groups, congregations, etc., not as individuals. All need
to have some shared *values* around equality, justice, freedom,
human dignity, fairness. The broad-based character is to give the
organization strength across political, geographical, religious,
and racial divides; to provide solidarity – a creative and positive
alliance able to make a powerful challenge.

Second, broad-based organizing is *issue-based*. It is multi-issue
and does not deal with universal problems, but rather breaks
major problems down into manageable, specific issues. It sets
realizable goals. Tactical decisions are made to tackle winnable
issues – ones which are local and over which people with power
(in local authorities, business, etc.) can be made accountable. The
broad-based organizer will have a strategy team which has to
listen to the authentic concerns of the local community and
decide what goals are realizable.

Third, it is based upon *collective leadership*. The paid organizer
works to discover the real local leaders – those with untapped
potential, with the capacity to influence others – to give them
training. There is not a single charismatic leader, but a rotating
leadership model. Leaders share responsibility and are answer-

able to the groups, so that the leadership is properly representative of the grass roots constituency and the organization fully *owned* by its membership.

Finally, *self-interest* is an underlying assumption of the broad-based organizing method. This is not selfishness or self-centredness, but a recognition that 'no one is an island' and working in isolation will not achieve change.

The advantages community organizing has over UK-based community development may fall into the following areas:

- the techniques of developing a community organization are detailed, pre-planned, and pragmatic
- they do not rely on a haphazard, individualized community worker's perceptions of what he/she feels is right
- the framework of relationships, once developed, provides a solid foundation, built on understanding how the members are motivated
- the development of a structure of power allies reduces the likelihood of being marginalized or being categorized as 'loony lefties'
- community organizing is pragmatic and not an ethereal ideology with no practical methodology
- community organizing is effectively managed with an agenda of action relevant to the community. It is not 'worker-led'.

Community organizers in the United States often acknowledge that the approach developed by Alinsky and refined by the IAF is distinctively American. In a 1984 study, James Pitt and Maurice Keane analysed the cultural, political and religious differences between the United States and the United Kingdom and concluded that 'it is absurd to think that Alinsky-type organizing could, or should, be transferred to Britain. It developed in a particular country and context and must be understood in the context.' Other British writers, while acknowledging the difficulties of shifting the IAF's style of organizing across the Atlantic, conclude that community organizing holds tremendous promise for Britain.

Alinksy's work is now influencing community work in this country. The withdrawal of many community services in Britain is a clear political decision, and the struggle for very scarce resources has to be conducted at the political as well as the local community level. Given the track records of groups in Bristol and on Merseyside, the idea is up and running. Community organizing is here in Britain and it is working.

If organizing is to thrive in the United Kingdom over the long term it will have to confront the distinctive challenges that the British context presents: feebler churches, centralized political power, a weaker democratic tradition, and the need to develop a coherent ideology for organizing within the existing tradition of community development. In the wake of success in Merseyside, along with that of its sister organization in Bristol, several Anglican dioceses and the Church in Wales are committed to developing broad-based organizing in their regions, and work has already begun in Sheffield, the Black Country and in east London under the auspices of the Citizen Organizing Foundation.

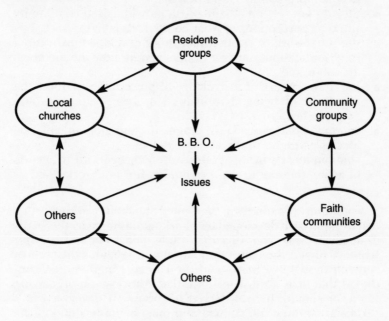

Broad-based organizing

Community ministry

The most persuasive way to encourage churches to take the implications of community work into their systems is to establish a concept of 'community ministry'. In its publicity the Southwark Anglican Diocese talks about the need to recognize that local churches belong to two communities: their own community of the faithful; and local and national communities of which the

churches are an active, if somewhat marginalized, part. The
Southwark community ministry pack says it is about:

(a) recognizing different sorts of community

   • neighbourhood – sharing area and resources and 'being
     in the same boat'
   • community of interest – the local church, the community
     of faithful Christians, local and national organizations,
     work associations, interest and pressure groups, etc.

(b) affirming that the local church belongs to both sorts of
    communities, sharing and responding to the joys and sorrows
    of its members and its neighbourhood. The interface
    between this understanding of community and ministry is
    community ministry

(c) understanding different sorts of shared ministry

   • supporting church members in their growth in faith –
     study, worship, reflection, teaching
   • pastoral care of individuals both within the church family
     and outside it
   • maintenance and development of people, plant and systems
   • evangelism
   • involvement in issues of justice and peace, social action,
     community development, developing church projects
     and the use of church buildings
   • ordained ministry.

Ann Morisy, a worker in the London Diocese, holds the view
that community work and community development undertaken
by the churches can be seen as an 'unconditional gift' from the
churches. She says that many workers would bristle at the
thought of their work being seen as part of a process of 'softening
up' by the churches. Community ministry, she argues, allows the
distinctiveness of the churches' contribution to community work
to be owned and understood. It makes a link between community
work, community development and pastoral ministry.

The churches, through their undertaking of community audits
and their experience of engagement in a variety of projects, have
a responsibility to confront those responsible for community care
with the analyses and conclusions of this work. This must be done
through using the sociological and theological tools of analysis
which the churches have as their own particular area of expertise.
All this must be done from a base within the local church, and
must be fed back into the churches and into the lives of
worshipping congregations. Ann Morisy says 'Community
ministry requires active pastoral care to be a part of a church's

daily ministry. Unless someone hears day-to-day the cry of those who are grieving, isolated or anxious, there is no platform for community ministry.' When pastoral care and community ministry are located together at the heart of parish life, pastoral care ceases to be a quiescent, repetitious response of the local church to the needs of individuals. It becomes a point of discernment, a research tool, and a prompt for a purposeful, corporate response.

Conclusion

The way in which community work is undertaken needs to be carefully planned and vigorously examined before it is begun. The definitions of community care, community work, community organizing and community ministry which have been set out here are a beginning. They arise from understandings contributed by those active in the field at the moment. Because all good community activity involves a dialogue between partners, this debate about definitions will continue.

Involvement by local Christians and churches in the lives of their various communities is essential. It is a natural out-working of the demands of the Gospel. There can be no doubt that because of their massive investment in this work, the churches have a major contribution to make, both in their understanding of justice in society and from their experience as practitioners in the field.

THE PATIENT APPROACH

What I like most is the patient approach.
You know, the one that says.
I know I won't change the world
With what I'm doing
But it's worth it
To help one other human being.
Urban Poems, The Kairos Group

CASE STUDY
The community newspaper

I have been involved for some time in the running of a community newspaper on the GLC estate where I am working as a clergyman, but with a community development function. I initiated the newspaper with other clergy working on the estate eighteen months ago.

I tested out the idea whilst visiting members of the estate when I first arrived, and it seemed that it would be appreciated. I agreed to act as editor. Following a meeting with the Community Development Officer and members of the community we managed to gather a small staff to run the paper, as well as a large group who were willing to distribute it to various roads on the estate.

I am now rather worried because it is seen as my paper, even though members of the community contribute quite a lot. Thus, when the paper raises issues of concern to the community, members of the local council find it difficult to distinguish my views from the views of the estate, and this reduces the value of the paper. I have therefore been aiming for some time to slide out of the editorial chair, but so far have failed to do so.

Could I have avoided this problem, and if so, how?

CASE STUDY
The unsupported mothers' group

A community worker in a very deprived working-class area got some unsupported mothers to come together for a meeting with her. Once there, the mothers decided to continue meeting in order to discuss some of their common problems, such as low income, lack of social life, being mother and father to their children, etc. The meetings were well attended, but although individuals attended, many mothers had pressures which prevented regular attendance.

Initially the mothers tended to look to the worker to carry out tasks for them. She resisted, except for offering secretarial help through her office. Between meetings she visited those who had not been able to attend the previous meeting, and encouraged an active member of the group to undertake similar visiting.

The worker was a bit worried because the members appeared unwilling to take on any formal responsibility. They also did not appear to want a formal committee structure (although some members had visited a group in a middle-class area which was run on very structured lines).

In many respects the worker felt that the group had made progress in five months since it first met. It had organized regular meetings; a second-hand clothes swap-shop; and coped with having to change its meeting place. It had also advertised its meetings in the local press and drawn in some new members, including some unsupported fathers. The workers saw the encouragement and support offered to the men encouraging in view of the bitterness the mothers had expressed at early meetings about 'typical masculine behaviour'.

In spite of all this the worker feels that the group has not yet 'gelled' and is therefore disappointed. Could she achieve more if she worked differently?

Further Reading

Neighbourhood Care in Practice, Rodney Hedley (LVSC, 1984)

Definition of Community Work (Federation of Community Work Training Groups, 356 Glossop Road, Sheffield S10 2HW)

The Non-Directive Approach, T. R. and M. Batten (Avec, 1988)

The Church and Community Development, George Lovell (Avec, reprinted 1992)

Churches and Communities, George Lovell and Catherine Widdicombe (Search Press, reprinted 1986)

Community Organizing? You've never really tried it?, James Pitt and Maurice Keane (J. & P. Consultancy, Birmingham, 1984)

Community Ministry: Linking private faith to public action, Ann Morisy (Avec Occasional Paper No. 1, 1992)

Community Organizing: A practical and theological appraisal, Jay McLeod (Christian Action, 1994)

3

Making a Start

Churches become involved in community work and community projects in a wide variety of ways. If the work is going to be done more effectively and if grants are going to be applied for, then the words 'management' and 'planning' take on a great importance. There is a wide range of support and help available for those wanting to expand a local piece of work or for those who feel it is right to begin a project as a result of conducting a local survey. So, the first sensible step is to consult this support network.

Local consultation

It is very likely that the voluntary organizations in any area are linked together in some kind of network. In towns and cities there will be Councils of Voluntary Service. In rural areas there may well be a Community Council. In smaller towns and in parts of cities there is likely to be a Volunteer Bureau. In each case there will be a staff member or a local organizer who can give help and advice. The Red Cross, the WRVS, the Children's Society and sometimes Barnardo's will have similar advisers or fieldworkers.

Even after the cut-backs, local authorities have local staff who may also be consulted. Many Social Services departments have a volunteer co-ordinator or adviser. This person may also be skilled in providing sources of training for volunteers and project staff. Hospitals also have volunteer co-ordinators. Depending on the nature of your concern or project, consultation will save hours of time in searching for advice and may well give access to otherwise unknown sources of help and funding. It may perhaps even give rise to new partnerships.

Consultations within the churches

Ecumenical developments among the mainstream Christian churches have led to the establishment of the Churches Community Work Alliance. It is part of the Council of Churches for Britain and Ireland. The CCWA has regional groups, and any community work staff would need to be linked in with their local network for support and training.

Depending on the denominational structure, each church will have a regional adviser on social issues. Titles will vary in diocese, district or province but a common title for such a person would be Social Responsibility Officer or Adviser. Urban and rural areas may have separate people.

The Church Urban Fund provides grants to local projects and churches in areas of deprivation. You will need to get in touch with the Diocesan Adviser who will help you with your application and will, in many cases, provide useful planning advice. This person will need to be contacted at an early stage if an application to the CUF is to be considered.

So, rule 1 is *consult*. After that begins the detailed process of planning and managing your project.

Aims and objectives

The words 'aims', 'objectives', 'goals' and 'targets' are often used rather loosely and sometimes interchangeably. They each mean 'what we want to do or achieve'. Their different uses often refer to the timescale involved.

Aims An aim is an overall, long-term goal; what your organization would achieve if it were 100 per cent effective. It defines why the organization exists, its purpose or reason for being. Nowadays it is also sometimes called an organization's mission and is expressed in a Mission Statement.

Objectives These are what an organization wants to achieve within certain time periods. All of an organization's objectives – whether long, short or medium-term – and all its activities should be in line with its aims or Mission Statement.

Types of planning

Strategic planning is for the long-term attempts to give a broad overview of the piece of work or project and looks at where it will fit into a wider plan.

Tactical planning describes the steps needed to implement a strategic plan or to achieve long-term goals.

Recurrent or cyclical planning requires preparation for events or activities which occur regularly or must be undertaken regularly.

Project planning is for specific, time-limited pieces of work.

Operational planning is to keep the organization or team functioning properly.

Day-to-day planning is for specific activities which need to be done immediately.

Contingency planning makes provision and allowances for the unforeseen.

Crisis management

This involves dealing with one crisis after another, rather than planning for them and trying to minimize the risk of them occurring. Even when crises are adequately handled this does not reflect good management. The reality is that most crises are not unpredictable – they can be anticipated and planned for.

A planning strategy

A strategy is a plan aimed at helping you to reach goals and objectives. In a structured way you will be able to move towards long-term aims. The following three plans are necessary if your strategy is going to be effective:

Development plan: sets out what the organization or church wants to achieve over a long-term but fixed period. It will involve negotiating and setting out a series of proposals to bring development, change or adaptation.

Strategic plan: examines and describes how the different elements in a development plan will slot in together. It will also describe the implications or costs in terms of time, money, people, equipment and premises.

Business plan: sets out projected costs for the organization's activities, anticipated income and from what sources, cash-flow – when income will come in, set against when payments have to be made, and financial requirements to cover rents, capital equipment and contingencies.

The action spiral

Running a project, like running any business, is a dynamic activity. The pace of it, the ensuing anxiety and the exhilaration of putting ideas into practice are all part of the genuine enjoyment – and exhaustion – of being involved in an innovative and pioneering piece of work. The action spiral shown here describes well the activities needed to initiate, run and renew a piece of work.

Based with permission on *Just About Managing*

Projects often have phases of dynamic activity or a 'life cycle' which can look like this:

- assess current needs, pressures, demands at a particular point leading to the demand for new developments
- review, clarify and confirm activities with reference to core purpose or Mission Statement
- collect opinions and new information
- revise short-term planning
- implement new or revised plans
- monitor new activities and achievements against short-term targets

- monitor against long-term objectives
- review and evaluate, leading to an assessment of new needs.

Finance and funding

Many church pieces of community work have small beginnings. They will be staffed entirely by volunteers. Funds will be donations of small amounts of money from churches or the local Lions or Rotary Clubs or other community organizations. Much equipment will be donated and very many resources will come in an unrecognized way from the volunteers or their friends. Often premises will be given free of charge, including the cost of heat and light, or offered at a very low rent.

Many things will force change upon such a small voluntary group. The most rewarding reason for the need to change is the success of the work: there are simply too many people wanting to attend and the volunteers and resources cannot cope. Needs will also have been identified through current work.

Another reason for the necessity of change is the implication of health or employment regulations. Increasingly, legislation is preventing informal voluntary activity. Food has to be prepared in ways, and in kitchens, which conform to hygiene regulations. Young, old or disabled people can only be accommodated if the building, the toilets and the equipment meet certain standards.

Finally, fatigue may occur among volunteers or a key, unpaid leader leaves and no replacement is available. All these factors will force the busy, successful, small project to need to attract larger amounts of funding to allow its work to continue.

Local authority funding

It is the policy of central government and of local authorities to try to care for people in their own homes as far as is possible. It is also policy to stimulate local voluntary action to enable a partnership to exist with 'professional carers'. This situation is a difficult one for voluntary organizations to live with as more and more demands are made upon them.

This concept of partnership, however, does mean that grants for a whole range of caring projects begun by voluntary agencies are available. Applying for local authority grants is a complex, frustrating and time-consuming activity. Negotiations need to be begun with local officers but frequently contact and lobbying with local councillors can help. Help will depend on the type of project you are developing and the local colour and policies of your council.

Local authority grants often only come once a project is up and running, when it can demonstrate its viability. This means that start-up money is needed for at least the first year of any major new initiative.

Charity funding

Many major national fund-raising initiatives have begun in recent years. Children in Need and the television 'Telethons' are often fruitful sources of initial funding.

For one-off donations, to get a local piece of work started, it is frequently profitable to send the project's local community representative from 'the great and the good' to speak at a Rotary or a Round Table meeting. Town mayors often have a particular charity for their year and they can also be lobbied or approached. 'Profile-raising' is important if a project is to get public support.

General letters to charities are unhelpful. Carefully worded and targeted appeal letters are important and more successful. Many national charities have local staff who can advise on funding. The Children's Society or Save the Children Fund organizers can be most helpful in discussing local funding.

Offers in kind

There are a range of sources of local labour available to help with repair of buildings or the provision of equipment. Local courts, in conjunction with the Probation Service, can award Community Service Orders of up to 100 hours to young people and adults as an alternative to a custodial sentence. Weekend 'work groups' or individual placements, with an agreed supervisor, can be a genuine source of help and a real piece of community involvement. Many companies and organizations may be reluctant to give money, especially to church projects. However they may well be able to offer equipment if you have a carefully targeted 'shopping list'.

The Church Urban Fund

This major Church of England charity was established in 1987 and has been making grants since 1988. Over £18 million has been raised and will be spent over a period of twenty years. It is a direct piece of action, arising from the report *Faith in the City*, of the Archbishop's Commission on Urban Priority Areas which reported in 1985. To avoid any confusion in interpretation of the policies of the Trustees of the Church Urban Fund, guidelines

for applicants and details of the Fund in the rest of this chapter
are taken directly from the Fund's own briefing papers, produced in 1993.

The Church Urban Fund:

- is for those in our cities who are poor, disadvantaged and feel
  excluded from the mainstream of our national and Church
  life
- arises out of the Church of England report *Faith in the City*
  and assists work that addresses the fundamental issues raised
  in that report
- is a practical demonstration that the Church as a whole is
  concerned for, and stands with, the deprived
- aims to help the people of deprived urban communities find,
  and implement, ways of meeting the spiritual and material
  needs of their own communities. It helps locally based
  projects and initiatives
- works in two ways: it makes grants to projects from its own
  resources; and it provides a vehicle for sponsorship and
  support by corporate and Trust donors.

To be eligible a project must:

- aim to assist people in a parish or parishes containing or
  falling within an area recognized by the Fund as an Urban
  Priority Area (UPA)
- have charitable purposes
- have significant involvement of the local church or churches
- be approved by the diocesan bishop and submitted to the
  Trustees by him.

Some projects will not be eligible:

- paying ordinary stipendiary clergy
- projects and activities for which funding is normally available
  from the Church Commissioners, dioceses, local authorities,
  statutory bodies, or organizations for the conservation of
  historic buildings
- grants to individuals
- direct support to other grant-making institutions
- capital support to Voluntary Aided Schools eligible for
  statutory funding.

The CUF prefers projects which:

- build on the existing presence of the Church

- demonstrate ecumenical working or work with people of other faiths
- are clearly managed by and/or employ members of the local community
- are directed towards areas of particular deprivation
- are innovative but of a long-term nature
- exemplify good practice and are likely to be repeated elsewhere.

Current priorities are:

- breaking new ground in evangelism or pastoral care in a way appropriate to UPA life ('new' means not the traditional clergy role)
- opening up church buildings or other resources to wider community needs
- addressing the major problems of the area – housing, unemployment, poverty, dislocation of social structures
- enabling local communities to organize, train or develop themselves
- addressing other problems of the area in a way which brings something uniquely Christian to bear; something the Church particularly can offer
- improving the Church's relation to the neighbourhood.

What is an Urban Priority Area

An Urban Priority Area is an urban area with multiple deprivation and can be either in the inner city or on an outer estate. *Faith in the City* describes these areas as 'districts of special disadvantaged character. They are places which suffer from economic decline, physical decay and social disintegration.' Six main statistical indicators are used:

Unemployment: percentage of economically active residents who are unemployed.

Overcrowding: percentage of private households living at more than one person per room.

One-parent families: percentage of private households containing one-parent families with dependent children under sixteen.

Lone pensioners: percentage of private households comprising one pensioner living alone.

Lack of basic amenities: percentage of private households lacking exclusive use of bath and inside WC.

Ethnic origin: percentage of residents in household of which the head was born in the New Commonwealth or Pakistan.

These statistical indicators – with that on unemployment given double weight – are combined into a single index. There are recognized exceptions, but in general the higher the score, the greater the level of deprivation. Dioceses are asked to establish which are their UPA parishes using these data. CUF grants are normally only available for projects in UPAs.

The UPA indicators form the basis for the Trustees' discussion. Other factors are taken into consideration, for example changes such as higher local unemployment rates which have developed since 1981, when the indicators were created. The 1991 population Census has brought a wealth of new statistical information and has forced a revision of the understanding of the way in which deprivation is measured and described. Church Urban Fund Link Officers in dioceses will have the latest information on how statistical information can be made available. Other information about how to use the new indicators can be obtained from the Church Urban Fund.

Applicants should consider the following questions, if appropriate:

- Is the project going to make any difference to the lives of the people in the area?
- Is it likely to achieve its objectives?
- Is the project earthed in its parish or community?
- Should it really be getting funding from elsewhere?
- Has the decision to do this been based on any knowledge of what is needed, or what else is available, in the area?
- Is this a conventional pastoral job in disguise?
- If opening a building to use by the community, is the project giving the community a share in the management of what happens, if appropriate?
- Have the applicants consulted any relevant sources of advice?
- Is this training, or giving experience in an area, which will enable people to get employment afterwards?
- Is it ecumenical?

- Has this scheme grown out of any specific biblical or Christian study?

All applications must be supported by the diocesan bishop. Applicants should contact their Diocesan Projects Co-ordinator or Link Office who will advise them on the local procedures for applications.

Grants

(a) Grants will normally be between £1,000 and £100,000 in total value. The Church Urban Fund will always require money to be raised locally in addition to its own grant, so as to show local commitment to and responsibility for a project.
(b) Partnership support from third parties (local authority, commercial sponsors and other charitable organizations) is strongly encouraged.
(c) While a grant may be something up to a 90 per cent of the overall cost of the project, the typical level is 40–50 per cent. Proposals for a higher percentage grant are looked at critically.
(d) The Fund may support the employment of staff for up to five years. A review will usually be made after three years, while applicants are free to reapply for funding in years 4 and 5.
(e) Funding after five years certainly cannot be expected. The Fund will look into applications for evidence that thought is being given to future funding or that the objectives of the project can be achieved during the life of the grant.

The employment of staff is a serious affair and it is recommended that these issues be dealt with:

- an equal opportunities recruitment policy
- a written job description
- a contract of employment
- clear management structure
- payment at the rate for the job
- reimbursement of working expenses
- the development (or otherwise) of the post, once the initial funding period has been completed.

(f) All grants are 'cash' grants and will, therefore, not be index-linked. Applicants should ensure that the appropriate increase in salaries or building costs are reflected in the application.
(g) Salaries for staff are paid quarterly in advance; capital costs are paid on receipt of copy bills, invoices or architects'

certificates for the work involved. The Fund does not require grants to be taken up in the year within which they are awarded.

(h) All payments are made on the understanding that the elements of the project specified in the submission approved by the Trustees will not be fundamentally altered, either in theory or in practice. If such a change occurs, it will be necessary to seek the Trustees' approval before further payments are made.

(i) In normal circumstances the Fund will not finance the payment of debts incurred on committed loans nor debts arising through poor financial management.

(j) The Fund has a system for monitoring and evaluating projects that it supports. Successful applicants will be given further information.

Full details of the Fund's work can be obtained from The Church Urban Fund, 2 Great Peter Street, London SWIP 3LX (Tel: 0171 (071 until 16 April 1995)-222 7010/Fax: 0171-799 1829).

In addition to the Fund's own staff the Anglican bishops have an officer, based in Church House, Westminster, who has responsibility for continuing to support the dioceses in the implementation of the recommendations of *Faith in the City*, along with subsequent policy developments.

A check-list for grant applications to any Trust

1. Make sure your application complies with the terms of the Trust.
2. Fill in the application form clearly and simply. Do not overload the Trustees with detail.
3. Speak to someone at the Trust by telephone to establish a personal contact.
4. Encourage someone from the Trust to visit and see your work.
5. Be clear about the amount of money you are asking for. Check that your figures add up.
6. Enclose all the papers and back-up information required – annual accounts, project aims, annual report, business plan for new project, references if needed.
7. Find out the dates of Trustees' meetings and submit your application in good time.
8. Demonstrate other support and describe what you will do if you are not awarded the full amount.

9. Do not ask for, or expect, continuation funding if the Fund/
   Trust clearly says it will not give it.
10. Try not to compete with other projects for the same money –
    community work is about demonstrated co-operation.

Do not give up

Fund-raising is a time-consuming and frustrating task. However
much help you may feel you are getting, you may still be
disappointed when the Trustees of a charity or a council
committee meet and decide against you. As a general rule, the
more you negotiate with a Trust secretary and keep to the
guidelines of the Trust, the more likely you are to get a grant. All
applicants are competing in a shrinking market but do not give
up. When successful you will be even more aware of the
opportunities now available to you, and the responsibility you
have to make the very best use of the money.

RIGHTS

I got rights, you got rights
We all got rights and we exert them.
He say my rights they is wrong
He say I cannot express them.
My man he stand up for me.
Together we too strong for him.

Different voices, conflicting voices
Who can find a path between?

There are times when I am critical and bitter.
And times when I am full of love.
If my moods swing between these divisions
Then who I am to judge?
Urban Poems, The Kairos Group

CASE STUDY
The International Year of the Child and the itinerants

The Roman Catholic parish in which I work has a Parish
Council which is purely advisory. This means that the priest
can test out ideas with the Council and the Council can

can test out ideas with the Council and the Council can make suggestions, but the parish priest has the final say. However, as all the Council members are involved in parish activities their ideas and suggestions are very often carried. It meets three or four times a year.

The Council has twelve members, made up of representatives from each parish organization, elected by their organization, the assistant priest and the parish priest as Chairman. I am the assistant priest in the parish and as such a member of the Council. I often put matters on the agenda and sometimes I am responsible for making the agenda.

At our Parish Council meeting in January, according to my normal custom, I put forward an item for the agenda (after discussing it with the parish priest). I suggested that the parish should do something special to mark the International Year of the Child. To set the scene, I prepared a hand-out on the subject so as to remind or inform those present about the Year of the Child, its aims and origins.

The parish priest asked me to introduce the topic when the item on the agenda arose. I referred to the hand-out which they had all read. I had given a good deal of thought to the subject and so proposed that we might think about children on our own doorstep rather than those out in, say, India. I observed that it is often easier to collect money or do things for children far away than for people in need in our own area.

I mentioned the children I had in mind: 'the itinerants' in the caravan site quite near the church. The site is lacking any facilities; children are living in damp and cold conditions and are knee-deep in mud; and there are no educational arrangements. I felt we could or should do something to help. I said this could be a practical project for us to celebrate the International Year of the Child.

The proposal was discussed by the members and these were some of the comments: 'Gypsies damage property and are a general nuisance . . .'; 'The Social Services help them anyway . . .'; 'You can't help that sort of people . . .'; 'Gypsies are better off than ourselves . . .'.

I then mentioned that I had recently spoken to some of the people from this site. They told me how unwelcome they felt in the church because, after making their way through the mud in the site, they were not presentable to well-dressed people in our church.

The general opinion was that we couldn't really do anything about this matter and so the subject was dropped and we moved on to other items. I still feel that we, as a parish, should be doing something about the International Year of the Child and the itinerants. Where do I go from here?

Further Reading

Alliance News (Churches Community Work Alliance, 82 Swan Gardens, Erdington, Birmingham B23 6QG)

4

Managing a Project

So, you have a grant! You have either been successful in obtaining extra or new money from your local authority, or a government department, or the EC, or you have been successful in gaining a grant from a national charity. All the hopes the planning group had when they filled in detailed application forms and had meetings with councillors or Trust secretaries can now be put into practice. The time has come to put together a structure which will contain those people who will manage the project, and which will give an opportunity for many others to feel involved. This chapter deals with organizing, and the individual responsibilities within, such a structure. For much of this information I have drawn heavily (with permission) from *Just About Managing* by Sandy Adirondack.

Once a management structure is established and money is in an account, then work may have to be done to buildings, equipment purchased, staff appointed and volunteers organized.

What is management?

Good management is a vehicle which will ensure that people give their best to and get the best from an organization. It exists to ensure that an organization can do what it wants and needs to do without wasting precious time, energy and money.

There is an aura around management which makes it seem like something people can only do if they are highly trained, extremely efficient or experienced in business administration. Nearly everyone is involved in management of one kind or another. Anyone who can get children up, fed, off to school and themselves off to work is a good manager. Anyone who has to organize a meal for a large gathering is a manager. It is also often said that anyone who can survive on Social Security is a good manager! What managing a piece of work in the voluntary sector requires is the confidence to transfer the experiences of managing in our everyday lives to new situations.

One way of defining management is:

> Ensuring an organization makes the most effective and efficient use of resources in order to achieve agreed objectives.

Who manages?

Every organization has a governing body which is legally and financially responsible for its activities. If the governing body is a Board of Trustees it is likely to delegate its day-to-day management responsibilities to another group who may be called a Management Committee or an Executive Committee. A management structure in a voluntary organization of any kind is likely to have a structure like that in the diagram on p. 56.

The Management Committee

The main responsibilities of a Management Committee or other governing body are:

- to maintain a long-term overview of the organization and all its work
- to make strategic and major decisions about the organization's objectives, policies and procedures
- to ensure the needs and interests of relevant people and bodies are taken into account when making decisions
- to ensure adequate resources (especially people and money) to carry out the organization's activities
- to monitor progress towards objectives, and other work
- to take legal responsibility for the organization and all its actions (or inaction). If the organization gets into legal or financial trouble, members of the Management Committee or other governing body can in many cases be held *personally liable*.

A Management Committee carries out its responsibilities by:

- ensuring people within the organization are clear about why the organization exists, its overall objects or purposes, and constitutional or legal limits on what it can do
- setting policy, and ensuring it is implemented
- setting strategic or long-term objectives (what the organization wants to achieve over, say, five to seven years for a large national organization, or three to five years for a smaller local group), and ensuring they fit into the organization's aims

| **Governing body** |
| Trustees   Board of Directors |
| (in a charity)   (in a company) |
| **MANAGEMENT COMMITTEE** |

↓

| **Delegated authority from the governing body** |
| **MANAGEMENT COMMITTEE** (if separate from governing body) |
| **EXECUTIVE COMMITTEE** (officers and others) |
| **ELECTED OFFICERS** (chair, vice-chair, treasurer, secretary) |
| **SUBCOMMITTEES or STANDING COMMITTEES** (permanent) |
| **WORKING GROUPS** (temporary) |

↓

| **Responsibility for all aspects of day-to-day management** |
| **SENIOR MANAGER** (chief executive officer, director, general secretary, manager, co-ordinator, etc.) |

↓

| **Responsibility for specific aspects of day-to-day management** **May have direct links with elected officers, subcommittees, etc.** |
| **LINE MANAGER** (Project, term or department heads, managers or co-ordinators; supervisors) |

↓

| **Responsibility for managing own work** |
| **WORKERS** (paid employees, volunteers) |

Based with permission on *Just About Managing*

- setting medium- and short-term objectives and priorities, and ensuring they fit into the organization's policies and long-term objectives
- deciding whether to undertake new projects or activities, and making policy relating to them
- interpreting or adapting policy when existing activities change
- helping the managers, staff and volunteers determine how the organization should carry out its activities
- ensuring there are proper procedures for monitoring and evaluating provision and use of activities, services and facilities.

Good practice·

Members of the Management Committee will be concerned that a project or piece of work is being carried out in accordance with its constitution, and that good practice is being implemented in the decision-making procedures and in the employment of staff. Specific responsibilities may include:

- serving a well-informed, interested, supportive Committee
- maintaining democratic procedures and accountability
- holding meetings regularly, and ensuring members have the information needed to make decisions
- calling the Annual General Meeting and ensuring elections and other essential items are dealt with as required
- ensuring adequate communication between the Committee, subgroups, managers, staff, volunteers, and the organization's users, members, clients, residents and other people served by the organization.

In addition to its constitution, an organization may have other rules or standing orders which set out how meetings are to be run, how decisions are made, when and how subscriptions are set, or other procedural matters. These rules should be kept with the constitution, and if necessary the appropriate sections of the constitution should be cross-referenced to the specific rules.

Legal obligations and undertakings

Statutory obligations exist in law and must be met. For example, an organization must register under the Data Protection Act if it keeps information about recognizable living individuals on

computer; similarly, it must give contracts of employment to staff
who work sixteen or more hours per week. It is the responsibility
of the Management Committee or other governing body to
ensure that these obligations are met.

Legal undertakings are legally binding commitments which the
organization chooses to enter into: for example, renting premises, hiring staff, leasing a photocopier or entering into a
contract to provide services. It is the responsibility of the
Committee or other governing body to ensure the organization
can and does meet the terms of any such undertaking.

Financial responsibility and accountability

The Management Committee or other governing body is responsible for ensuring the organization has enough money to carry
out its work, meets its financial dealings, and does not get into
financial trouble. This includes not only the payment of bills but
also ensuring proper records are kept and the organization's
money is spent in the correct way. This means the Management
Committee or other governing body has ultimate responsibility
for:

- wages, tax, National Insurance, statutory sick pay and mater-
  nity pay, pensions, redundancy pay, and any other pay or
  benefits due to workers under legislation or the terms of their
  contracts
- mortgages, rents, rates
- all other bills
- ensuring the organization will have enough money to meet
  any financial obligations when they come due
- ensuring all grants or other funds received for specific
  purposes are spent as specified
- ensuring the organization is being paid enough for any
  services it is providing under a service agreement or contract
- ensuring the organization's funds are wisely invested
- ensuring the organization keeps accurate and comprehensive
  financial records, accessible to Management Committee
  members and authorized members of staff
- receiving regular financial reports in a form which Committee members can understand
- ensuring annual accounts are drawn up and audited in
  accordance with the constitution and, where relevant,
  funders' requirements and/or legislation.

Employment and volunteers

In most voluntary organizations the Management Committee or other governing body is legally the employer, with responsibility for hiring, supporting and, if necessary, firing staff. This can cause all sorts of problems, especially if the Committee is made up of users or clients who receive services from the staff whom they hire, or comprises people who are not very aware of what the organization is doing. Even if some aspects of employment are delegated to staff or a personnel subcommittee, the Committee as a whole is responsible for ensuring the organization has appropriate procedures to:

- draw up and regularly update job descriptions
- ensure adequate funding to pay staff
- advertise appropriately, short-list, interview and select staff
- issue and abide by contracts of employment
- ensure there is appropriate induction, training, supervision, support and, ideally, a regular review/assessment procedure for staff
- deal with moans and grievances
- undertake disciplinary and redundancy proceedings.

If some or all of the organization's work is carried out by volunteers the Committee has legal responsibility for them and their work. The Committee should ensure that they are adequately inducted and supported, and that there are appropriate disciplinary and grievance procedures. If a staff member or volunteer acts negligently, for example by giving incorrect advice to a client or not looking after a child properly in a community nursery, members of the governing body could be found negligent if the organization does not have and enforce proper procedures for recruiting and training staff, setting standards, monitoring work and maintaining a safe environment.

Equal opportunities

It is the responsibility of the Management Committee or other governing body to ensure the organization complies with equal opportunities legislation (Race Relations Act, Sex Discrimination Acts, Equal Pay Act, Disabled Persons Acts). But good practice goes far beyond the legislation. If the organization is concerned about equal opportunities (and all voluntary organizations should be) it is the Committee's responsibility to ensure the organization has a clear statement of intent on equal opportunities and a workable code of practice setting out how it will make its statement a reality. Further, it should ensure the code of practice is implemented and monitored.

Adapting and using buildings

Few buildings are 'tailor-made' for the needs of a project. On the contrary, it is more likely that the building will need a considerable amount of adaptation to meet the requirements of a project and the demands of legislation, which must be met before the public can use a building.

The best way to begin to understood regulations and requirements is for members of the Management Committee to consult those with specialized knowledge. The local authority will advise on planning requirements and what permissions will be needed before a building can be adapted. The Social Services department and others from the local authority will be able to advise on what a building will need: ramps for wheelchairs; handrails for the disabled or elderly; toilet facilities for toddler groups or the disabled; and the whole range of regulations regarding kitchens, hygiene and food storage. Often a wider group of Church Trustees will need to be consulted.

An architect's advice may be invaluable. It may be possible to get informal advice at an early stage. Later, if drawings are needed, then the architect's fees will need to be included in the capital costs budget. Much work can be done on a building by volunteers but imaginative ideas can be gained, and often expense saved, if expert advice is sought at an early stage.

Management check-list

The diagram opposite may help as a check-list for the management tasks of managers and of Management Committees.

Charitable status

Any organization in England and Wales, whether unincorporated or incorporated, can register as a charity with the Charity Commission if all its aims and objectives are charitable, and all its activities are 'charitable' or are allowed under charity law. In Scotland and Northern Ireland charitable organizations apply to the Inland Revenue for charitable status.

Charitable organizations are not obliged to register with the Commission, but those which are not registered are less likely to be able to get the tax and other advantages of charitable status. However, some charities have the benefits of charitable status

STRATEGIC MANAGEMENT
Provide direction and leadership
(for organization, project, team, department)

Develop overall policies and ensure implementation
Develop and sustain vision
Develop new ideas
Strategic planning and development

Ensure clear achievable shared core objectives
Ensure adequate resources
Ensure appropriate communication and decision-making
Monitor and evaluate work against objectives
Ensure appropriate communication and decision-making
in all these processes

MANAGE THE PEOPLE
WHO DO THE WORK

Recruitment and selection
Encourage teamworking
Appropriate information and consultation
Appropriate involvement in decision-making
Ensure appropriate skills and knowledge
Training • Supervision
Monitor performance
Acknowledgement/praise
Personal support

MANAGE
THE WORK

Set clear, realistic targets
Ensure adequate resources
Planning
Good systems and procedures
Time management
Clear standards and
expectations
Monitor quality and quantity
of work
Improvement and change

DO THE WORK
In small organizations
managers may also do the
work of the organization.

All workers are
responsible for
self-management.

MANAGE
INFORMATION
AND COMMUNICATION

Evaluate ideas and information
from outside organization/team
Evaluate ideas and information
from inside
Organize information
Communicate appropriately
Store information

MANAGE
EXTERNAL RELATIONS

Liaison with other
organizations/teams
Liaison with funders/donors
Represent organization/team
Publicity
Public relations

MANAGE
MATERIAL RESOURCES

Manage premises
Manage equipment
Manage materials
Manage stock

MANAGE FINANCE

Financial planning (budgets)
Financial monitoring
Financial control
Manage funding and funders
Manage fundraising

WHAT MANAGERS DO

Based with permission on *Just About Managing*

without registering with the Charity Commission. Places of worship, Scouts, Girl Guides and very small charities are exempted from having to register. Organizations with charitable purposes registered as friendly societies or industrial and provident societies are also exempt from having to register.

There are only four types of recognized charitable activity. They are:

Relief of poverty: helping people who are 'poor, ill or disabled, or aged'.

Advancement of education: education or research for the benefit of the public, including arts and sports facilities.

Advancement of religion: religious activities which benefit the public (not just members of the church or religious groups).

Other purposes beneficial to the community: other activities, such as providing public recreation and leisure facilities or promoting racial harmony.

All registered charities must have Charity Trustees (sometimes called Management Trustees) who have ultimate responsibility for the organization. In some charities the Trustees delegate some management responsibilities to another body, which might be called a Management Committee but does not have ultimate responsibility. In this situation the relationship between the two groups must be clearly set out in terms of reference. Serious problems can arise if the Trustees and a subsidiary committee do not know what each other is doing or disagree about what the organization should do.

Charity Trustees cannot 'profit' from the charity. This means they cannot be employed by the organization, even for part-time or temporary work. Conversely, employees of a charity cannot be a Trustee and cannot be voting members of the Committee if the Committee is also the Trustee body. (Employees can, of course, attend meetings and participate, if the Trustees so wish.) If the charity wants to give grants or financial benefits to individuals who are on the Trustee body (for example, an AIDS charity giving a grant to an HIV positive person who is a Trustee of the charity), advice should be sought first from the Charity Commission.

Most charities must submit their accounts each year to the Charity Commission, and to the Inland Revenue if they want to claim the tax benefits which charities enjoy. Under the Companies Act 1989 a charity which is also a company, and which does not have the words 'charity' or 'charitable' in its name, must indicate that it is a registered charity on its business letters, notices, cheques, orders, invoices, receipts and all other official or financial documents. The Charities Act 1992 extends this obligation to charities which are not companies.

The Charity Commission can advise on any aspect of charity registration or charity law, and should be contacted if there is any doubt about what a charity can and cannot do. *Responsibilities of Charity Trustees* is a free video and nine-page booklet from the Charity Commission: charities should distribute this to all Trustees. The Commission has a wide range of other free material on all aspects of charity registration and administration. The Commission's addresses are:

St Albans House, 57–60 Haymarket, London SW1Y 4QX (Tel: 0171 (071 until 16 April 1995) -210 4477) for national charities and charities in London, the South East and East Anglia.

Graeme House, Derby Square, Liverpool L2 7SB (Tel: 0151 (051 until 16 April 1995)-227 3191) for charities in the Midlands, Wales and the North.

Woodfield House, Tangier, Taunton, Somerset TA1 4AY (Tel: 01823 (0823 until 16 April 1995)-34500) for charities in Southern and Southwestern counties.

Officers and their responsibilities

Although there are broad similarities, the exact role of the elected officers is different in every organization and at different times within the same organization. The organization's constitution may set out officers' basic responsibilities, but how they carry these out and what additional responsibilities they take on will depend on a number of factors. These might include the individuals involved, the sort of work the Management Committee does, and whether there are paid staff. It is important that everyone on the Committee understands what officers are supposed to do in their organization.

The Chair

The Chair's role has two separate parts:

- planning and running meetings: being sure everything is covered and decisions are made when required, keeping order, helping the group to deal with differences of opinion and conflicts, being sure everyone who wants to has a chance to speak
- ensuring the organization as a whole sets and sticks to its policies and priorities, serving as a spokesperson for the group, making essential or emergency decisions between Committee meetings, helping workers deal with difficult situations.

The first role can be rotated, although it is good practice to give everyone two or three meetings in a row, rather than just one, so they can learn from their mistakes. The second role should be taken for at least one year by a person elected at the Annual General Meeting or chosen in some other formal and democratic way. It is not good practice to rotate or change the organization

Chair at intervals of less than one year. A constitution or rules may limit the Chair's tenure to a fixed number of years, to be sure no one stays in the post too long.

If urgent decisions must be made between meetings, the organization's constitution or rules usually give the Chair the right to take action. This should be used only for decisions which genuinely cannot wait. If the organization's policy on an issue is not clear the Chair should consult with the Vice-Chair or others before proceeding. Any action taken under Chair's direction must be reported to the next meeting of the relevant group.

The Vice-Chair

The Vice-Chair stands in for the Chair and helps with difficult decision between meetings. Sometimes the Chair deals with the 'organization' and policy side of chairing and the Vice-Chair with the meetings side. The Chair should liaise regularly with the Vice-Chair and ensure s/he knows enough about current issues within the organization to be able to stand in at short notice.

The Secretary

The Secretary's role also has two distinct aspects:

- helping the Chair plan meetings: ensuring they are held according to the constitution, ensuring notices of meetings or agendas are drawn up and sent out in advance, if required, and members receive all necessary information; taking and distributing minutes; helping the Chair ensure decisions are made when required
- dealing with correspondence, ensuring the appropriate people are notified of correspondence, sending out publicity or other information about the organization.

The roles can be divided so that a Minutes Secretary deals with meetings and a Correspondence Secretary deals with letters.

If the organization is a company limited by guarantee it will have a Company Secretary whose duties are defined in law. An organization with a Company Secretary does not have to have an elected Secretary as well, but can do. The division of responsibilities which lie between Company Secretary, Minutes Secretary, Correspondence Secretary and staff must be absolutely clear. An industrial and provident society also has a Secretary with defined duties.

Treasurer

The Treasurer must ensure the group spends its money correctly, pays all its bills and does not get into financial trouble. The Treasurer must also ensure the Committee receives regular financial reports and has enough information to make decisions about finance. The full responsibilities of a Treasurer are described later in this chapter.

Collectives

Groups which work collectively or non-hierarchically have to deal with particular issues:

- workers sometimes think that by cutting out managerial and supervisory staff the need for the work undertaken by those staff is also eliminated
- 'self-management' may be interpreted as meaning individual workers are entitled to do whatever they want whenever they want, so long as they report at some point to the staff or team meeting
- anyone who takes managerial responsibility may be seen as authoritarian or anti-collective, so no one initiates anything until the situation becomes impossible
- 'collective management' may be interpreted as meaning all workers have to be involved in all decisions all the time, or even have to agree with all decisions all the time
- the Management Committee may be drawn into the anti-management ethos, and may be unable to make effective decisions for the organization

Under these circumstances collective working may seem satisfactory in very small, informal groups where objectives and philosophy are clearly defined and agreed. But unless the problems are dealt with, collective working is likely to be virtually impossible in larger groups or in groups where there is disagreement about objectives, priorities or standards.

Collectives have the same management responsibilities as other organizations; the only difference is that those responsibilities are *shared among workers* rather than being attached to specific positions in the organization. In groups which work collectively or non-hierarchically, the responsibilities which managerial and supervisory staff carry out in traditionally structured organizations must be undertaken by the staff or team meeting. The meeting may, in turn, decide to delegate some responsibilities to specific people, either permanently or on a rotating basis.

Management Committees in collectives have exactly the same responsibilities as Committees in traditionally structured organizations. As in any organization some Committee responsibilities may be delegated to staff but the overall responsibility and legal liability remain with the Committee or other governing body.

An excellent analysis of one agency's positive experience in developing collective working practices is *Invitation to Self-Management* by Alan Stanton (Dab Hand Press, 1989; Dab Hand Press, 90 Long Drive, Ruislip, Middlesex HA4 0HP).

Managing money

Put simply, managing money means

- not taking on obligations the organization cannot meet
- being sure the organization has enough money to pay its bills on time
- actually paying the bills on time
- keeping proper records of all money received and spent.

Financial responsibility involves keeping records ('accounts' or 'books') of how much money has come into the organization, where it has come from, and how it has been spent. This process is called bookkeeping. Along with the books, the organization must keep documentation, such as invoices or receipts, to prove the money was spent in the way shown. The books and documents will be used to draw up regular monthly and/or quarterly accounts, financial reports (sometimes called management accounts) and the annual accounts. The books and financial documentation must be kept for seven years.

Even when an organization acts responsibly and keeps all the necessary records, it may have problems with its accountability. This means being clear about who has the right to know what the organization is doing with its money, and how much control those people have over financial decisions. Legally, the Management Committee or other governing body is responsible for the financial undertakings of a community group or voluntary organization. (If the organization is a charity, the Trustees will have this responsibility. Usually the Trustees are the same as the Management Committee.) To make proper decisions, the Committee or Trustees need adequate and comprehensible information about:

- the group's budget (what it expects to receive and spend during a fixed period or for a specific project)

- its cash-flow projection (when it expects the money to come in and go out), and how any shortfalls will be covered
- its income and expenditure (what it actually receives and spends)
- its assets (the value of what it owns, and money owed to it)
- liabilities (what it owes).

Staff or volunteers with responsibility for bookkeeping, financial administration and/or financial decision-making are always accountable to the Treasurer, and through the Treasurer to the finance subcommittee (if there is one) and the Management Committee or other governing body as a whole. The Committee is, in turn, accountable to the membership if it is a membership organization, and must provide accounts to the members each year. A good Committee will go beyond this, ensuring the accounts are presented in a way members can understand, and providing opportunities for members to ask about them.

Legal responsibilities and taxes

If an organization is a limited company it must send audited accounts annually to the Registrar of Companies. The accounts are kept on file and are available to the public but, unless there is a complaint of fraud, the Registrar will not question them. Industrial, provident and friendly societies must send audited accounts to the Registrar of Friendly Societies, who check the accounts to be sure funds have been properly used.

An organization registered as a charity must send its accounts to the Inland Revenue if it claims any of the tax benefits charities enjoy. The Charities Act 1992 requires all registered charities which are not registered as companies to keep accounts, have them independently examined or audited, and submit annual accounts to the Charity Commission. (Charities which are also companies are already required, under company law, to prepare a full set of accounts and have them professionally audited.)

For charities which are not also companies, the type of accounts and audit depends on the charity's annual income:

Income up to £25,000: a simplified receipts and payments account, and statement of assets and liabilities must be prepared. The accounts must be examined by a qualified auditor or 'an independent person who is reasonably believed by the Trustees to have the requisite ability and practical experience to carry out a competent examination of the records'.

Income between £25,000 and £100,000: a full set of accounts (in accordance with the Charities Act regulations) must be prepared, and must be examined by a qualified auditor or an independent person.

Income over £100,000: a full set of accounts must be prepared and professionally audited

Unregistered charities with an annual income of less than £1,000 must prepare simplified accounts; unregistered charities with income over £1,000 must follow the same rules as registered charities. Slightly different rules apply to exempt and excepted charities.

The Charity Commissioners may at any time scrutinize any charity's accounts, to be sure the charity's funds have been spent in accordance with its aims and objectives and that no funds have been spent for purposes not allowed under charity law. If funds have been misused the Commission and Inland Revenue can remove the privileges of charitable status from all the organization's funds or from funds which have been used for purposes the Commission judges to be non-charitable.

An organization must register with the Inland Revenue for PAYE ('pay as you earn') if it:

• pays workers, even on a casual basis, who earn more than the minimum National Insurance (NI) threshold
• pays workers, even on a casual basis, who work in another job as well (even if they earn less than the NI threshold in either or both jobs).

The organization must deduct tax and National Insurance from the earnings of all workers who earn more than the tax/NI thresholds, and this deducted amount is paid to the Inland Revenue every month. PAYE records must be kept for a least three years.

If an organization receives income from sources other than grants, donations, subscriptions and investments it may need to register for Value Added Tax (VAT) if this income is more than the VAT threshold. This applies even to charities. Specialist advice is always required when dealing with VAT, as it involves keeping very detailed records.

Grants and donations are not subject to corporation tax but organizations which receive income from other sources such as trading or property rents, may have to register for and pay this tax. Charities which reclaim tax on covenanted donations must also keep special records.

Details of accounting requirements for charities and other voluntary organizations are available from the legal department of the National Council of Voluntary Organizations, Regents Wharf, 8 All Saints Street, London N1 9RL (Tel: 0171 (071 until 16 April 1995)-713 6161).

Responsibility to funders

Any grant-aided organization should ensure it has, in writing, a statement of how much and in what way the funding body expects to exercise control over the grant. The organization should ascertain how much information the funding body wants, how often and in what form. It is important to be clear whether the funding body wants complete accounts or only accounts covering its grant; and whether it wants accounts quarterly, annually or on completion of a one-off project. The same principles apply to work paid for under a service agreement or contract rather than a grant.

If the funder demands a representative with voting powers on the Management Committee, clarify how much power that person has to take part in decisions not directly related to the funding. Clarify, too, what will happen if decisions with which the funding body subsequently disagrees are made when the representative is absent.

Treasurer's duties

In a small group, the Treasurer may deal with all aspects of finance and funding. As groups grow or take on paid staff, some responsibilities may be delegated to a volunteer or paid worker, or some may be shared within a finance subcommittee (if one exists). Even if the financial decision-making and work are carried out by the Treasurer, finance subcommittee and/or finance worker(s), final responsibility for financial matters always rests with the Management Committee or other governing body as a whole.

The Treasurer's responsibilities can be divided into six broad categories. The check-list below can be used to decide which tasks should be carried out by the finance worker or Treasurer, and which require the involvement of the finance subcommittee or other governing body.

General financial oversight

This category covers broad responsibility for the organization's financial decision-making. It includes:

• ensuring funds are used in accordance with the constitution and Committee decisions

- ensuring use of funds complies with conditions set by funding bodies
- ensuring workers and members of the Management Committee or other governing body know enough about financial administration, bookkeeping and the accounts to be able to do their work properly and make decisions for which they are responsible
- advising on financial policy issues: for example, what expenses can be claimed and the procedures for claiming them; the circumstances (if any) under which staff can receive advances on their salary payments; financial implications of new activities; or the organization's policy on charging for its services
- advising on contracts of employment (if there is no personally subcommittee), and on other contracts
- making financial decisions on behalf of the Management Committee between meetings, and reporting such decisions to the Committee as appropriate
- liaising with the bank or other financial institutions on behalf of the organization
- preparing accounts for audit, and discussing them with the auditor as required
- deciding on security measures to ensure cash or cheques are not misused.

Funding, contracts, fund-raising, sales

This area of responsibility involves ensuring the organization has enough money to carry out its activities. The sources of this money can be divided into funding (grants which are applied for from statutory authorities, Trusts and other sources); contracts or service agreements to provide activities or services; fund-raising (activities such as membership drives, appeals, jumble sales or special events undertaken by the organization or its members to raise money); and sales of goods or services.

   Responsibilities in these areas include:

- collecting and acting on information about statutory, charitable, business and other funding sources
- completing and submitting funding applications
- co-ordinating funding applications
- liaising with funding agencies
- drawing up tenders or proposals for contracted services
- co-ordinating fund-raising activities
- ensuring money received for special projects is spent for those purposes, and if necessary is separately accounted for

- ensuring goods or services to be sold are priced appropriately.

Financial planning and budgeting

The Treasurer has overall responsibility for financial planning, including:

- preparing budgets for ongoing work and special projects, in consultation with the appropriate workers and funders
- presenting budgets to the Management Committee or other governing body for approval
- keeping track of actual income and expenditure as compared to budgeted income and expenditure, and adjusting financial forecasts as appropriate
- deciding priorities, in case of cash-flow problems (not having enough money to pay bills when they are due), for paying and negotiating for late payment if necessary.

Financial reporting

The Treasurer is responsible for ensuring the Management Committee or the governing body has enough information to make its decisions. This means:

- reporting regularly, in writing, to the Management Committee on the organization's financial position
- preparing and presenting financial reports and accounts when required
- presenting the end-of-year financial reports (draft annual accounts) to the Management Committee or other governing body
- presenting the audited accounts to the Annual General Meeting
- ensuring members at the AGM have a basic understanding of the annual accounts and the budget for the current year.

Banking, bookkeeping and record-keeping

Although the Treasurer may not actually do the tasks involved in getting money into and out of the bank, or writing up the books, s/he is responsible for:

- advising on which banks or other financial institutions the organization should use and what type of bank account it should have (Note: every decision to open, close or change a

bank or other account must be approved by the Management
Committee or other governing body)
- serving as a signatory for the organization's bank accounts
  (all changes of signatory must be approved by the Management Committee or governing body)
- ensuring there are proper systems for receiving and paying
  out cash and cheques
- setting up appropriate bookkeeping and petty cash systems,
  and ensuring related documentation is kept
- ensuring membership subscriptions are collected and proper
  membership records are kept
- ensuring other moneys due to the organization are collected;
  that guidelines exist for action to be taken in cases of non-
  payment, and such action is taken if required
- ensuring receipts are issued, if required, for money received
  by the organization
- ensuring all income (including cash) is paid into the bank
- ensuring all bills are paid
- ensuring everyone handling money for the organization
  keeps proper records and documentation
- controlling fixed assets and stocks; these are valued annually
  at the time of stocktaking, and the balance sheet is revised
  accordingly.

Enlarging the small print

All these detailed descriptions of the duties of officers and the
legal obligations of Trustees may seem tedious to a group of
enthusiastic and often idealistic people who have just achieved
one of their greatest dreams. However, I have visited a number
of projects where Management Committees have found that they
have had to pay large sums of money to the Inland Revenue
retrospectively because they were unaware of the financial
responsibilities of employing staff.

Charity law has been tightened up considerably and much
careful detail has to be studied by someone involved with the
project if all the new responsibilities are to be carried out
effectively. Fortunately, all those who manage charities are in the
same position. Networking – of knowledge and of experience –
can be invaluable here. Good community work practice involves
projects and voluntary organizations pooling knowledge, especially of this technical and detailed kind.

CASE STUDY
The members' committee

A flourishing one-night-a-week club had a leader with a strong personality who decided almost everything without consulting the members. As things ran well the members were happy to allow this. Then the leader resigned on moving away from the district.

A new leader, who held strong views about members accepting a good many responsibilities in helping to run the club, said so from his very first night. This soon aroused the resentment of some members. When he realized this, the leader made direct approaches to those members with the strongest resentment and the situation 'warmed' a little.

When this happened the leader formed a small *ad hoc* Members' Committee drawn largely from this group of people. It was with this Committee that the leader raised the whole question of responsibilities in relation to running the club. He suggested that certain tasks such as canteen duties, collection of subscriptions and cloakroom rota should be taken care of by the members' committee.

Some rather half-hearted discussion followed and a few members of the Committee were pressed (by their fellow committee members) into accepting one or other of the duties. These duties were never taken seriously and chaos soon resulted. The leader began pressing the Committee to do something about it.

What went wrong?

CASE STUDY
The Over-60s threaten UDI

The new GLC estate in my country parish, within two years, had an active Community Association based at the community hall built by the GLC. It held a number of activities including an Over-60s Club meeting on a Thursday afternoon.

I became aware of increasing friction between the Club and the Association. The Secretary of the Association was accusing the Club of using Association sugar and bingo cards. The Club was accusing them of changing the plugs so that they couldn't use their own equipment, not making the key available to open the Centre, and interfering in their activities.

The Club decided to form its own Committee to raise and handle its own funds. The Secretary objected, saying that money raised by member clubs actually belonged to the Association. He told them that all members of the Club should also be members of the Association (at 5p a week for OAPs). This caused uproar among the Over-60s Club leaders and they threatened to make the Club independent and get their members to stop paying subs to the Association.

I felt that this would harm both Club and Association and that I should do what I could to improve relationships and prevent the split, or at least to get people to see the implications of taking this step. I shared my concern with a colleague, a community work student working on the estate, and we tried to work out what was the best thing to do. We decided to speak to the Association Secretary and his wife (who was Assistant Secretary).

We found them concerned to keep the Club going as part of the Association, but they felt it right that members should pay their subs to the Association as was the rule for all other member clubs. All he wanted was to look through the Club's membership book and see if most of them belonged. We asked them if they would be willing to meet us and the leader of the Club to talk things over. They were happy to do this. My colleague arranged with the Club leader to hold this meeting at a suitable time for everyone.

Again, my colleague and I thought carefully about what we should do and how the meeting could be handled. We felt they should try to talk about and face up to the deep, underlying feelings at the root of the problem. Accordingly, I opened the meeting by saying how well I thought the residents had done in setting up the Club and Association so soon after the estate was occupied, and that one would expect in such circumstances that some problems should arise. This particular problem seemed to have arisen because the people who ran the Over-60s Club had, at the time it opened, been very active in the Association. They then found they couldn't manage both, and had increasingly put their effort into the Club. The Club then began to stand on its own feet, but what started as a measure of independence turned into a deep split because of a disagreement on the Committee.

At this point the meeting started to fall apart. The Secretary said 'That's Committee business and not what we came to discuss', and one of the Club leaders said that she was the person involved in that disagreement and she felt the Secretary had treated her very badly over it. Furthermore, she said the Secretary had allowed £200 of Association money, most of it contributed by the pensioners, to be spent on making up the losses on a trip to Blackpool, and now the Association wouldn't let the Club have money to help run a party for the OAPs. The Association Vice-Chairman, who was also at the meeting, said he had come to discuss problems with the Club. He didn't think there were any Association problems and he didn't think what I had been saying was relevant – so could we get back to the subject.

I said I thought this ill-feeling was making a big problem out of a small one, which was that the Secretary felt he had a right to know if the Club members were paying their Association subs. 'He's not going to have our books', said the Club leader. After further discussion which cleared the issue about the key, the sugar and the bingo cards, and the plugs, the Club leader agreed to provide a list of members. The meeting ended quite amicably.

We left feeling we had made some progress, but in fact the list was never provided and the hostility of the Club leaders and the Association Secretary seems as great as ever. What could we have done differently? What should we do next?

Further Reading

Just About Managing, Sandy Adirondack (LVSC, 1992)

Voluntary But Not Amateur: A guide to the law for voluntary organizations and community groups (LVSC, 1992)

The Effective Trustee (Directory of Social Change, 1994; Radius Works, Back Lane, London NW3 1HL)

5

The Human Face of Management

For the effective management of a local community project it is essential that good communications are maintained between the project Management Committee and the main governing body of the local church. If the project is supported by, or originates from, a group of local churches, then the need for good communications is even greater.

Effective management is as much about the maintenance of good personal relationships as it is about the setting up of correct structures. It is quite possible to have a project with all the right things in place, all the correct procedures followed, all the accounts kept correctly, and for the project still be an unhappy place to work. Personal relationships are the cement which holds a piece of work together well or, if things are bad, it is the crumbly mortar which will allow cracks to show all to easily.

'Bite the bullet' is the best advice which can be given. Tension and irritants rarely just go away or resolve themselves. Frequently they get worse or go underground and surface as symptoms in some other way. Many who have studied the ways in which organizations work will say that the problems which people complain about are rarely the real issues. They are symptoms of some underlying, often structural, problem in the organization. Similar diagnoses come from family therapy. The 'problem child' is not to be seen as the real or only problem. Treating the child alone will not bring a permanent change to behaviour. The immediate family has to be dealt with if the underlying problems are to be brought to the surface.

Community projects as models

One of the exciting characteristics of very many community projects is that they are established with a high amount of idealism. Many of the mistakes which have been experienced in other organizations are deliberately avoided in attempts to establish new structures, sometimes of an experimental or radical kind, in the new venture. A number of important characteristics, listed below, require a mixture of organizational and personal 'chemistry' to bring about the desired change.

One-to-one relationships Space and time are deliberately pro-grammed in so that differences of personality can be explored. Often different personality type-indicators can be used in a sensitive way where appropriate. Such care can help people to understand why they find others difficult to work with. Often through this further understanding growth in personal relation-ships can take place, or at least people learn why they can or cannot work with others in the same group or team.

Group-to-group relationships It is an essential feature of community development work that different groups are able to communi-cate with one another. Projects will try to model this relatedness as a part of their good practice.

Project-to-church relationship This essential area of contact ensures that what can be a minefield of difficulty and misunderstanding can become an area of mutual learning. When a local congrega-tion experiences a good relationship with its community project it can gain confidence to go on to form good relationships and alliances with other community groups.

What you can hope for but not legislate about

When things go well certain characteristics are not talked about but do become evident in the smooth running of a project. They are immediately apparent to the visitor and can emerge at the time of an evaluation.

Trust emerges as a project develops. The experiences of coping with the ups and downs of everyday working life will either contribute to the building up of trust between individuals and groups, or the reverse. In a similar way, forgiveness, though rarely described as an event, will be experienced as workers look at how differences have been resolved and new working practices established.

Good judgement comes with experience. No manager, worker or volunteer will have the wisdom of Solomon on day 1 – or ever at all – but the patient carrying out of tasks and the dealing with a range of different and often difficult people will gradually build up the experience which leads to sensible judgements being made both about people and about the management of a project.

Professor Gillian Stamp has written about this in a most illuminating way in her article 'The enhancement of ministry in uncertainty':

> When more and more time at work has to be given to engaging with uncertainty, either because there is no time to gather the information required, or because it is not available, a different kind of skill is called for. And that in turn calls for a person, not a computer. The skill in question is judgement – 'what you do when you don't – and can't – know what to do'. For this, people turn inward to a resource that they describe as 'sixth sense', 'gut-feeling', and that they know they should trust – 'it's when I don't trust it . . . when I let the "facts" sway me, go against it, it's then I make a mistake.'
>
> These descriptions are not new. The nineteenth-century philosopher John Locke spoke of 'the faculty which God has given man to supply the want of clear and certain knowledge in cases where it cannot be had, is judgement . . .'. And a contemporary writer on social institutions pointed out that 'work is the exercise of discretion within prescribed limits in order to reach an agreed goal . . . while knowledge is one of the essential tools of work, it is not the work itself . . . in work, knowledge alone will not see you through . . . in work you are confronted by problems that have no absolutely correct answer. You have to use knowledge and judgement in interaction.'
>
> So, systemic wisdom in an organization – working with the grain of the dynamic system of which it is a part – rests on the best possible use of people as makers of decisions and members of a group with a shared sense of purpose and direction.

The local vicar, priest or minister

'Never let the vicar chair your Management Committee', said one group of workers and Committee members. They were expressing a particular kind of exasperation. It arises from the dual role of the relationship a minister has within a local church and often within a project. If the priest is the Chair of the Management Committee then the role is one of authority and carries with it some executive responsibilities. These might often involve the making and carrying out of difficult decisions causing pain and unhappiness. This role may well conflict with that of being 'friend' and 'pastor' to those in the project. Some clergy can live with the tensions of this dual role and resolve it very well, others find it a constant source of anxiety. When these two different roles do not have clearly observed boundaries then many in a project become confused and some get hurt.

I helped to run a one-day conference at which members of Management Committees, project workers and clergy were present. One important point made by all except the ministers was that they themselves do not present a very good role model for community workers to follow. Clergy work long hours, do not take their time off, and sometimes neglect their families and friends. They may well be fulfilling their calling as they understand it but they are not demonstrating the best way in which those in charge of their own time and diaries should operate.

These points are made not to prevent clergy being central to the establishment of projects. They are a warning. In practice, many projects would not have come into being were it not for the entrepreneurial activities of a local minister. Projects succeed because one person has a vision, can mobilize others around it, and is available through the weekdays to give time when needed.

Probably one of the greatest difficulties for clergy is to know when to move away from central activity in a project. Ministers are only in part community workers. One of the greatest skills they can develop is that of enabler, working non-directively to give others the self-confidence to take on more responsibility. Priests and ministers are also likely to move every five to seven years. It is never fair to expect their successors to have the same interests or to be prepared to take on the same community responsibilities. It might be sensible advice for clergy who are central in the management of projects to give themselves the aim of withdrawing from leadership within three years and moving to a role as 'adviser' or 'chaplain'.

The issues raised in the discussion above relate also to other difficulties which Christians are thought, rightly or wrongly, to have over management responsibility. Some of these are in the areas of dealing with conflict and with stress.

Managing conflict

In any group there will be differences. People think differently, have different values, interpret information in different ways. Differences are the basis on which individuals, relationships or organizations grow and change. Sameness may seem attractive but it leads, in the long term, to complacency and stagnation. In effective organizations or teams there is a shared sense of unity, of commitment to common objectives and ideals, but there is also a shared sense of diversity. Differences are welcomed, there are clear opportunities for people to express and discuss their differing views, and people are committed to finding ways to operate which value everyone's contributions and beliefs.

This does not mean everyone can always get what they want. People must recognize they are working together as a group. Sometimes they may have to do things they do not want to do, go along with decisions with which they do not fully agree, or even, if the group goes in a completely unacceptable direction, sever their connections with the group.

Conflict arises when differences cannot be satisfactorily dealt with. Differences become conflict if:

- people are unwilling to accept the validity of different values, priorities or views of what is 'right' or 'important'
- individuals or the group as a whole have different or unclear standards for action, behaviour or performance, and common standards cannot be agreed
- something (money, attention, workload, responsibility) is, or is perceived to be, unfairly distributed
- people feel an individual or collective need to win, be right, get their own way or dominate
- people succumb to fear, distrust and the need to define anyone different or unknown as 'other', 'outsider' or 'enemy'
- the people involved do not want to change
- there are unclear or non-existent procedures for discussing and resolving differences before they escalate into conflict.

When problems, disagreements or conflicts arise people's first response is usually to define their own position. Conflict resolution is then seen as a process of negotiating among the defined positions to find a solution to the immediate problem.

That kind of conflict resolution is important. But it is more productive, in the long term, for the whole group (not just the people directly involved in the conflict) to look beyond the presenting problem to underlying issues and confusions. The most common underlying issues can be divided into four broad categories:

- policies, objectives and priorities
- inadequate resources to meet needs or demands
- structures and procedures
- personal, historical and hidden issues.

Exploring these underlying issues takes time and commitment, but it can make it easier to deal with the presenting problem and prevent related problems from arising. It is, of course, even better to sort out what the group is doing and how it is doing it before problems arise.

For Christians there may be the extra temptation to try and avoid or ignore differences. There is no reason to suppose that

Christians will be especially favoured with the absence of difficulties in their work. In fact, problems in projects managed by Christians may be made even worse if conflict and problems are avoided. It is often the best pastoral approach in management to face a problem and deal with it as soon as it is seen. To be firm and decisive early on in a difficult situation may well save many people being hurt if a problem is left to drift. Difficulties rarely go away and if they are forced underground only emerge again in a different guise.

Managing stress

The other problem workaholic Christians frequently have to face is stress. Within work settings, probably the most useful definition of harmful stress is changes in a person's physical, mental or emotional condition, or in behaviour, caused by constant pressure to perform in ways which are incompatible with perceived or actual ability, time or resources.

There are no easy answers in dealing with stress. People have to decide what is right for them, and what they are willing and realistically able to do. The basic guidelines are:

- recognize and acknowledge what is causing the stress, without pretending, making excuses, or blaming someone or something else
- recognize and acknowledge present and potential effects
- decide whether you (not someone else, but you) can do something to change the situation
- if you cannot (or are not willing to) change things, decide whether you can (and are willing to) change the way you react to it, for example by not getting so angry or hurt about it
- decide whether you can (and are willing to) reduce the negative effects of stress on you, for example, by taking time to relax so you are not so tense
- if you really cannot (or will not) do anything to change the problem causing the stress then accept it, because worrying about something you cannot or will not change only makes it worse
- decide what you can realistically do to help yourself manage or cope with the stressor or its effects by setting realistic, time-limited objectives and getting as much support as you can
- do it
- keep yourself strong and relaxed: allow yourself to relax (long baths, music before bedtime), give yourself treats and incentives, say no to anything that would increase the

pressure, and don't punish yourself if you don't do as much as you intended.

For Christians, stress can be caught up with feelings of guilt about the responsibility of trust given to you in a project. It is easy to feel you are letting people down and not living up to the high hopes everyone had at the beginning of a piece of work. Problems are rarely one person's fault, and corporate responsibility is as important as corporate planning and decision-making. Scapegoating or putting all the blame or stress on one person is all too often an avoidance of real responsibility.

The often quoted prayer by Reinhold Niebuhr can become the solution to stress — but only after the responsible manager or committee Chair has been through the fiery furnace of experience. Stress goes with any responsibility. Some people thrive on it, others are not happy unless they are really worried, some should never undertake the responsibility of managing others at all.

> God grant me courage
> to change the things I can change,
> the patience to live with
> the things I cannot change,
> — and the wisdom to know the difference.

The human problems of success

Difficulties which arise in the management of a project are all to easily seen as yet another series of problems rather than as the inevitable consequences of success. If a real need is being met and if volunteers are able to work well together, then expansion and an increased workload are inevitable. The problems of success will have some of the following characteristics.

Volunteers become paid staff While good news for the project and for someone who will begin to earn a salary, there are bound to be tensions as all involved adjust to new roles. If one of the volunteers is appointed to a paid post, while delighted, that person will definitely find difficulties in establishing a new working relationship with old friends. The former volunteer may have to begin to supervise those who were on the same informal footing until the appointment was made. Friction is likely to occur and a careful watch needs to be made by the Management Committee, or one person designated from it. Perhaps an outside consultant can be brought in.

When a person takes up a paid appointment for the first time in the history of a project there is also the 'temptation' for both other volunteers and the Management Committee to 'give up'. The work of setting up a project is completed, now all those who have worked so hard to set it up can have a rest. The paid worker can now do the job!

What has actually happened is that a project has reached a certain stage in its life. Quite probably new skills will be required for the next phase. It is appropriate for some volunteers and for some members of the Management Committee to 'bow out gracefully', without any sense of frustration or failure. Very many people in community work are there because they like the informality of it. They are 'people people' not 'structures people': a larger and more complex organization will not be for them. It is a mistake to stay on too long, however deep the emotional attachment to a piece of work. People can easily feel let down or even 'betrayed' as work moves on in new ways. Regular users can also feel that their old friends are no longer so available. Managing change also involves providing good exit routes for those who want to go – and for those who need to go for the sake of the development of a project!

The professional worker A trained community worker or youth and community worker will come into a project with new ways and ideas. Those who were delighted that an appointment has been made may soon feel disillusioned when they see the directions in which the worker may want to move a project. Local volunteers may also be surprised that the worker will want to establish a less personal – more impersonal – more professional relationship than that of a group of friends, who in the past had been willing to do almost anything and work any hours to keep the project going.

The new worker will also want professional support. This will need to be established both for the worker in an independent way and also within the Management Committee so that there is someone there who will understand the methods and approaches that the worker is bringing to the project.

Managing large amounts of money The Treasurer who is happy collecting small amounts from members and the occasional £25 or £50 from a donor may well feel overwhelmed by the scale of finances in a developing piece of work. The technicalities of employing a person and calculating amounts of tax and National Insurance may be quite beyond the abilities of the honorary Treasurer, who is really just one from among the original group of volunteers. Either special training needs to be offered or a kind way found to let that person step aside.

The potential for worry and confusion when finances get out of control is very great. The line between incompetence and mismanagement is hard to draw. Fortunately, many funders will want to be assured that a project can manage its finances adequately before a grant is made. This scrutiny is good discipline to ensure that a responsible Treasurer is appointed.

Training for all involved With the tremendous amount of experience of community work which is now available, it is not necessary for people in each project to have to find everything out for the first time. Much human suffering and anxiety can be avoided if advice and training are given to staff and to members of Management Committees. Regional groups exist in almost every part of Britain and Ireland where significant amounts of community work are being done. These groups offer local support and training. Each denomination also has an adviser and offers pieces of training. Agencies are also available as a resource. Church Urban Fund small grants are now available for training, but the best advice is to budget an appropriate amount of money into your funding application at the outset.

People grow and develop One of the most rewarding aspects of many pieces of community work is that those involved grow as people when their horizons are broadened and as they take on more responsibility. A particular human problem for managers is that not all of those they work with or supervise will be developing at the same pace. Within the spectrum there will be those who are so energized by a developing piece of work that they will be pushing for more and more to be done and will almost seem to be a threat to staff and managers. Others will move at a slower pace and will be testing out their own ceiling of responsibility. Sensitivity to individual needs is essential if conflict is to be avoided.

Some users will also be seen to be developing and this is especially rewarding. However, by the very nature of their handicap or disability some users will seem to remain relatively the same over the years. There may be an element of frustration among project staff when this seems to happen, even when greater resources have been put in and better facilities are available. To be stable in a secure environment is progress for many users, where before they had been familiar with a lifetime of trouble and regression. Project staff may need to recognize and accept different levels of progress and stability as they present themselves.

Special training and counselling may also need to be provided for those working with the elderly. Bereavement is going to be an inevitable feature of this work, and here churches and clergy can be particularly helpful. Most appropriate and thoughtful funeral services can be put together when family, project and church combine to honour a life bravely lived.

People matter

The bedrock of any piece of community development work worth the name is that people are taken seriously. The human face of management for a project is much more than just a slogan. Personal relationships between all those involved in a project, and between groups, is fundamental to the development concept of the work.

Structures are designed quite deliberately with people in mind, and are devised and revised with the intention that people will grow and develop. As with any other company or small business, size and growth bring their own problems. How these human-sized questions are understood and resolved is yet another contribution which well-managed pieces of community work can make to our understanding of the ways in which people behave within organizations.

CASE STUDY
The parish soup kitchen

Mrs C, one of my parishioners, moved by compassion for the down-and-outs, took soup and sandwiches *in situ* where she could find them. There was no provision for them in the town. Subsequently she got permission for the use of an old shed, in the grounds of the church, as a soup kitchen. It's open every Sunday evening.

Mrs C has largely financed it herself, and she had a few loyal helpers. I have supported her soup kitchen through-out, both with moral support and money. One of the parish organizations offered its help, which she accepted, but she complains about their ineptitude at talking to the 'clients' – but also complaints about lack of help!

Recently the Town Hall has taken an interest in the vagrant problem and set up a working party, which is exploring a possible hostel project. I was invited to join the working party, which I did. I did not suggest Mrs C because she is impossible in a group and talks everyone down.

The Probation Service has now offered to staff the soup kitchen on a second evening, a Monday. I agreed readily, as the Probation Officer is very interested in the problem, knows many of the clients and has young and eager helpers. Mrs C felt rather threatened by this and resents the Monday opening, especially as they provide better food.

She objected to their cooking on the site and threatened to close her Sunday operation. The Probation Officer has complained about the filthy state of the kitchen, and has offered to redecorate. Mrs C says it's not meant to be the Ritz: if it looks too smart it will spoil the atmosphere. And so on . . . There is a constant sniping, and I am forever having to keep the peace in order to prevent one or the other closing down.

Now the Probation Officer wants to lay on a Christmas dinner. It has always been Mrs C's proudest boast that she is the only person in the town who ever does anything for these people over Christmas: she has provided soup and sandwiches for them at a time when all the cheap cafés are closed.

What can I do to get some sort of harmony between these people?

6

Employing a Worker

One of the joys of a large injection of money into a project is that it enables a worker to be employed. This can raise a whole range of hopes about what might be achieved. It also offers the temptation for the Management Committee to relax and expect the worker to do much of what they had previously been doing themselves. One of the pieces of bad news about a cash grant is that it is usually for a limited period of time, often for three years. This means that, although a worker can be employed, there is always an element of insecurity in the appointment because long-term work cannot be guaranteed. For these reasons it is very important that the project Management Committee try to be as 'good' employers as possible and that firm agreements are made and written down. The seeds of discontent are often in the 'grey', unclarified areas surrounding an appointment.

Early plans

The first discussion needed is whether having a paid employee is the best way to develop the project. Answers are often clear because of the volume of work expected from volunteers, and also from the obvious potential in a vibrant and expanding project.

Advantages

- stability and continuity
- professional expertise
- a wider range of skills
- ability to organize and train volunteers
- a greater volume of work can be managed

Disadvantages
- large extra costs are incurred
- more responsibilities are placed on the Management Committee
- volunteers become confused about their role
- existing community leaders feel threatened

Finance and budgeting

There are more 'hidden' costs (but not optional extras) which come with employing a worker, even if that person is part-time. Here is a list of budget items which will need to be considered before a worker can be appointed. This outline of costing for a local project can be used for guidance. In drawing up a budget, expenditure can be grouped under broad headings, but different funders will have differing approaches to budget division.

Revenue budget

Worker costs
- salary (is it related to a scale?)
- National Insurance
- employer's pension contribution
- travel (including meals, if appropriate)
- training
- contingencies

Office administration
- postage and stationery
- telephone
- printing and publicity
- information resources
- contingencies
- maintenance

Premises costs
- rent/rates
- heating/lighting
- insurance
- cleaning
- equipment hire
- repairs and maintenance

Project costs
- insurance for all staff and volunteers

- volunteer expenses
- childcare for volunteers
- equipment maintenance
- new developments

Vehicle costs
- petrol/oil
- road fund licence
- insurance
- repairs
- AA/RAC
- depreciation

Capital budget

- desk/chairs
- typewriter and office equipment
- furniture
- telephone installation
- building works

Other setting-up costs

- recruitment and induction

Also ask: can the costs of any other activity be legitimately included in the project? This can be a way of meeting 'core' organizational costs.

Part-time appointments and job-shares

If the job is described as part-time or half-time, or for a specified number of hours per week, great care needs to be taken in accepting the honesty of such a time limit. Particularly in voluntary organizations, there is a great temptation to describe a job as part-time but to mean that much more will be expected.

Other jobs are limited in hours not because of the amount of work to be done but because of the amount of money available to pay a worker. If working hours are flexible then diaries fill up very rapidly. It is a great source of anger for part-time workers, and their partners, that the hours at work expand to look like a full-time job on half pay!

It is the responsibility of the Management Committee to ensure that this exploitation of a worker does not get out of hand. Workers can help themselves by getting some training in time management and by having a personal work consultant or supervisor.

The concept of a job-share is very attractive to many people. It gives the employer a wider range of skills in a post, and workers the opportunity for flexibility. Many of the dangers in part-time working also apply to job-shares, however. It is very easy for time to expand and for frustrations and misunderstandings to occur. Lines of demarcation and separation need to be agreed between job-share staff. Job descriptions should be reviewed when the two people have been in post for a few months, and also when one part of the share leaves.

Employers will find costs slightly higher with a job-share, and it is quite likely that more office space will be needed or more spent on facilities for working at home. Generally, the advantages of a job-share greatly outweigh the disadvantages.

Information on job-sharing and other flexible working arrangements is available from New Ways to Work, 309 Upper Street, London N1 2TY (Tel: 0171 (071 until 16 April 1995)-226 4026).

The job description

Applicants need to be given as clear as possible an indication of the range of tasks required in the job and the skills which will be needed to carry them out. A job description should include:

- job title
- main purpose(s) of the post
- accountability (to whom the new worker is responsible)
- supervisory responsibility (workers whom the new person will supervise or manage)
- main responsibilities of the job, with a detailed breakdown if this is appropriate
- a starting date, if this is fixed
- summary of the main conditions of employment including starting salary, increments, pension arrangements, hours of work, holidays, probationary period, arrangements for supervision and staff reviews
- closing date for applications, and dates of short-listing and interviews.

In the list of job responsibilities include only tasks that are genuinely part of the job. The job description should not be so complex that only a genius could do it, or so simplified that people apply for the job who are not able to do it.

Equal opportunities in employment

It is illegal to set requirements or use criteria which discriminate directly or indirectly against (or in favour of) people on the basis of their racial group, gender or marital status. Under the Race Relations Act 1976, 'racial group' includes race, colour, nationality, national origin or ethnic group.

Racial group, gender or marital status can be used as a factor in recruitment or selection only if it is a *genuine occupational qualification* for a job and can be justified in terms of the job description and task analysis. 'Improving the racial or general balance of the staff' or 'making the staff more representative' does not in itself constitute a genuine occupational qualification. However, if particular racial or ethnic groups, men or women are under-represented within the staff group it is legal to *encourage* people from those groups to apply for a job.

Direct discrimination means discriminating against (or in favour of) people specifically because they are of a particular racial, national or ethnic group, or gender. Indirect discrimination means setting criteria unnecessary for the job which disproportionately cannot be met by people of a particular group. For example, requiring GCSE maths (rather than requiring 'ability to keep simple financial records') discriminates against people who did not go to school in England or had to leave school early.

An organization of any size with a commitment for equal opportunities will also want to take into consideration the possibility of employing a person with a disability, unless it is genuinely apparent that they would not be able to carry out the job. The limits for applicants should be stated in the job description.

Free pamphlets and leaflets about the legal aspects of equal opportunities in employment are available from the Commission for Racial Equality, Elliot House, 10–12 Allington Street, London SW15 4EH (Tel: 0171 (071 until 16 April 1995)-828 7022); and the Equal Opportunities Commission, Overseas House, Quay Street, Manchester M3 3HN (Tel: 0161 (061 until 16 April 1995)-833 9244). Other free materials relevant to equal opportunities include:

Code of Good Practice in Employment of Disabled People, Employment Service, Rockingham House, 123 West Street, Sheffield S1 4ER

HIV and Aids: Policy guidelines for voluntary organizations and small employers, LAGER (Lesbian and Gay Employment

Rights), St Margaret's House, 21 Old Ford Road, London E2 9LP

Declaring Convictions: A guide to the Rehabilitation of Offenders Acts and applying for work with a criminal record, NACRO, 169 Clapham Road, London SW9 0PU

Advertising

Rule 1 is always advertise, even if you have a very good internal candidate. Advertising is expensive, however, so great care needs to be given to ensure that a maximum number of suitable applicants will know of the vacancy. Justice needs to be seen to be done.

Local papers are good places to advertise. For large jobs national newspapers may be considered. Papers which ethnic minorities read should also be used. If it is a church job then denominational papers can be used – but they are expensive. Allow at least three weeks between placing the advertisement and the date of the interview.

It often pays to send a letter around to local contacts, to other voluntary agencies and to local authority departments. Local shops and community centres will place the advertisement on their notice boards. JobCentres will also circulate other JobCentres.

The application form

You can use your own or adapt one from a similar organization. It needs to include:

- the applicant's name, address, phone number, date of birth, and any family details they want to disclose
- present and previous employment, with dates, grades/salary rates
- education, schools, colleges, qualifications
- names, addresses and phone numbers of two references, with a note at which stage they may be contacted
- details of voluntary work, previous appropriate experience, and hobbies and interests
- a short paragraph about why they think they are suitable for the job
- whether their present employer can be contacted, and the period of notice needed
- other relevant details – driving licence, typing and short-hand, ability to use word-processors (and which one!), any other languages spoken, any religious affiliation.

Short-listing

At least two people should be involved in drawing up the short list. A minimum number of those to be interviewed needs to be agreed beforehand. Regardless of which system is used, the final decision about which applicants to short-list is easier if each short-lister has been asked to use a simple code to indicate preferences on the short-listing form:

4: definitely interview
3: maybe interview, tending towards the positive
2: maybe interview, tending towards the negative
1: definitely not interview.

The interview

Candidates need good notice of the interview, the length of time they will be required, and how to find the interview venue.

The interview panel needs to agree the areas in which each person will ask questions. The Chair of the panel should take care of the layout of seating and be in charge of introductions. It is now normal to give applicants an opportunity to have a good look round, and to meet the staff. It is not always the case that other applicants are met.

Twenty to twenty-five minutes should be given to each candidate, with a five-minute break between each. At the end of an interview candidates should be asked if they have any questions. They should also be told how, and when, the result of the interview will be announced. Confidentiality within the interview room is essential.

It is often not a good idea to give detailed reasons for a decision to unsuccessful applicants. Some may be helped, though, with suitable advice and encouragement to continue looking for similar work. All references for candidates not appointed should be destroyed after the interviews are concluded.

Notifying applicants

If possible, the successful applicant should be telephoned to see if they would be willing to accept the post. It not, second and subsequent offers can be made. Once an offer has been made and accepted this should be followed by a letter, first-class post or delivered by hand, which will include:

• the date to begin work
• the salary

- details of three or six months' probationary time
- if the offer is conditional on a medical examination
- asking for written confirmation as soon as possible
- requesting the P45 form and National Insurance number.

Unsuccessful applicants should be notified as soon as possible, usually by letter.

Congratulations! You have made your staff appointment. However, the great temptation is to think your work is done. This is not the case. The task is changing, goals may need to be redefined, the new worker will need to be supported. Nothing is worse for a worker than to experience Management Committee, volunteers and supporters dropping out once they are in post because they think their work is done and someone new is being paid to take over. That is why a contract of employment is so important. The next step should be to clarify the staff contract.

A contract of employment

Employment legislation specifies that every employee who works sixteen hours or more per week is entitled to a written contract (statement of terms and conditions of employment) within the first thirteen weeks of employment. It is good practice to provide this contract for all employees, including part-time staff, as soon as they start work.

In management terms the contract is important because it should define clearly – for the employee, the manager and the Management Committee or other governing body – what is expected of the worker and the organization. These expectations should include:

- how many hours the employee is required to work each week; the extent to which individual workers can determine when they work, and the extent to which their times are set contractually or by a manager or staff meeting; whether flexi-time is allowed and, if so, whether there are core hours which must be worked
- whether overtime work is allowed; whether it can be paid or time off in lieu (TOIL) is given; if there is a maximum amount of TOIL that can be stored up, and whether it has to be taken within a specified period
- holiday entitlement (and how it is determined for part-time or job-share workers); how much notice is required to take time off for holidays, and whether notice has to be in writing or can be verbal; what happens if a worker falls ill on holiday; whether accrued holiday time can be held over from one year

to the next; what happens if the worker leaves while still owed holiday time
- whether additional time off can be taken for religious holidays other than Easter and Christmas, and if it is paid or unpaid
- arrangements regarding time off due to sickness, including whom to notify, maximum time allowed, what happens if that time is exceeded, and sick pay arrangements
- arrangements for compassionate or dependants' leave; whether there is a maximum that can be taken; and if it is discretionary, who decides what is allowed and whether it is paid or unpaid
- what workers should do if they have a grievance (complaint) or want to appeal against a disciplinary procedure
- how disciplinary matters must be dealt with.

A clear, workable contract, and an expectation that the conditions set down will be followed, can help prevent difficulties around poor timekeeping, excess time off and similar situations.

Contracts for volunteers

Volunteering is developing a professionalism of its own. A piece of work without any paid staff still needs to be done in as proper a way as if it had gone over all the hurdles of writing a job description and agreeing a contract. Many of those involved in volunteering will know that there are regulations and safeguards around voluntary work which compel references to be taken up and sometimes for police records to be checked.

Many of the more effective projects are now moving towards establishing contracts with their volunteers. These are written, agreed, and signed in a similar way to a formal contract of employment. Such a method has many advantages, not least that a piece of work done by a volunteer has a beginning and an end. Many are also relieved to know that there is a way of not continuing with an inappropriate volunteer.

Contracts for volunteers should specify the tasks to be done and the average time commitment which is expected. Such a written agreement can set standards and clarify an organization's position. It is also a useful document for appraisal or evaluation discussions. Contracts to regular volunteers should set out what the organization can offer (expenses, training, supervision and support, a reference if work is satisfactory) and what the organization expects (commitment to specific tasks and/or times, punctuality, confidentiality).

If things go wrong

Even with good supervision, review procedures and opportunities for training, some workers may still not perform adequately. What has gone wrong, and what can be done about it?

Inability to do the job

The worker may be incapable of doing the job or specific tasks within it. Can the difficult parts be done by someone else? Can the overall job be changed? Would additional training or support help? Can the worker be transferred to another post?

If there is at least one 'yes', the option should be explored. But if the answers are all 'no', the worker may have to go. Dismissal is highly unpleasant, and no one wants to be involved in it. Every effort should be made to avoid getting into a situation where dismissal is necessary. But if the work has to be done and the person cannot do it, it damages the organization, the person involved and the other workers to keep the person in post.

If an employee can be shown to be incapable of doing the work, the dismissal is 'fair' and the employee cannot bring a case of unfair dismissal against the organization.

Disciplinary procedures

Disciplinary action should only be started if informal discussions and supervision sessions with clear targets for improvement have proved ineffective, or if there is misconduct or a breach of rules which is too serious to be dealt with informally.

A disciplinary action is an important matter which affects the morale of everyone concerned: the worker, the manager, and colleagues. But it can be equally demoralizing if disciplinary action is not taken when everyone is aware that work is not being done properly or when a worker is constantly breaking the rules and being allowed to get away with it.

Every stage in the disciplinary procedure must clearly indicate

- what is wrong
- what needs to happen to make it right
- what the deadline is for improvement
- how improvement will be assessed, and by whom
- what will happen if the necessary improvement does not occur.

Disciplinary action relating to poor work performance is undertaken if informal chats and supervision sessions with clear targets for improvement have not produced the desired results. The disciplinary action usually starts with one or two verbal warnings. Even though these are called verbal, a written note should be given to the worker and a copy placed in the worker's personnel file. They should clearly indicate they are the first stage in disciplinary action. If performance does not improve, the next step may be more verbal warnings, or one or two formal written warnings.

Minor breaches of rules, for example consistent lateness which does not directly affect the organization's services to users, are usually dealt with in this progressive way. A more serious infringement of rules or policies, for example taking the organization's minibus without authorization, might start at the written warning stage.

If performance does not improve or rules continue to be broken, the next stage will be a final written warning, making it clear that dismissal may follow failure to improve. The worker must have the right to appeal.

An organization which regularly uses volunteers should also have a simple, fair procedure for dealing with disciplinary problems. This usually follows the organization's disciplinary procedure for paid staff but with fewer stages. The Volunteer Centre UK can advise.

Detailed information about disciplinary procedures is available from ACAS, 27 William Street, London SW1X 7AZ (Tel: 0171 (071 until 16 April 1995)-210 3000).

Dismissal

If the final warning is held on appeal to be justified, and if the worker's conduct does not improve sufficiently, the next stage is notice of dismissal. The employee must be given the amount of time specified in the contract of employment or the minimum time allowed by law. Alternatively, the worker must be given pay in lieu of this period of notice, if the organization does not want the worker to continue working during the period of notice. The worker must have the right to appeal.

All the disciplinary sections above can feel like very gloomy reading. There is a certain wisdom in setting up a project structure with the question in mind, 'What do we do if things go wrong?' Hopefully, if as thorough a preparation as possible is carried out before a project is begun and staff appointed, then the likelihood of things going wrong through confusion and misunderstanding will be lessened.

The church as an employer

One of the most difficult things for Christians, and for congregations, to cope with is a personal disagreement with a staff member or the failure of a project. Church groups are no more exempt than any others from difficulties in personal relationships or within projects. Indeed, Christians may be even more vulnerable if they fall into the trap of thinking that 'virtue is its own reward', and that with the divine guidance of the Spirit things will automatically go well. There can be no excuse for not ensuring that everything possible is done to support staff in their work, and to make sure that all those involved, volunteers and members of committees, understand fully what they are being asked to do and how much time and commitment is being asked of them. The idea that, because this is a church group, people will automatically be able to get on with one another and resolve differences all by themselves is nonsense and needs to be dismissed at the outset. Experience in other parts of church life should prove this point. The world we live in has demonstrated to very many that church people are by no means immune from conflict, trouble, failure and unemployment. Churches as employers in local projects do have a responsibility to try to be at least as good as other employers and, where possible, to demonstrate good practice in employment procedures.

Good practice can often mean having to be responsible and 'tough' as an employer. It is no help just being weak or 'nice' when a problem needs to be faced head on. Nor is it a responsible use of funds to allow an employee to take advantage of a church just because Christians do often find great difficulty in facing conflict. Letting things drift and avoiding difficulty can create even more problems for the future, often immediate problems for other staff and volunteers in a project, to say nothing of the lack of responsibility towards those who are being cared for or worked alongside.

Forward together

Most projects are success stories. They demonstrate development from small, often voluntary, beginnings to larger-scale pieces of work dealing with considerable sums of money. Much learning is done through the experience of shared work in setting up a project.

Stability and continuity are more assured if work is done *with* other people and groups. Community development work which achieves real and lasting results among all those involved is work which has drawn very many people and groups into a network.

The experience of learning to co-operate is one which will have brought real learning and growth to people and communities, and will have a long-lasting effect on all those involved. It will also demonstrate qualities required in a good voluntary organization employer.

A new chapter is opening, with the possibility of new partnerships with increased resources. New possibilities come on the horizon. Churchill said it well during the war: 'Let us go forward together.'

CASE STUDY
Working for interrelated development?

I am a community worker in a project on a large run-down housing estate. It was initiated by the Government five years ago and has been handed over to the local authority, which appears to be politically uncommitted to it. I work with both tenants and the local authority to improve the management of the estate.

I help the tenants to organize themselves through a now-established structure where elected representatives of the different areas of the estate have regular meetings, first with the tenants of the area and then with representatives of the local authority, mainly officers. I have an amicable relationship with the Senior Housing Officer, Sue, and the three Estate Officers and, indeed, work from a desk within their office. But I've inferred from them an intense dislike of the project as a whole.

Before one area meeting with tenants, I visited the four representatives to collect agenda items and discuss any concerns. Two of the four complained very strongly about the rudeness of one Estate Officer – Anne, who's been in post about a year. Although I don't trust John's objectivity I know he has a lot of influence on his block. Mary, who is known to be fair-minded, was reporting complaints from several others. Because I work in the same room as Anne, I know she is often both rude and unhelpful to tenants.

Although worried about the potential explosiveness of the issue, I decided it would be wrong to suppress it. I discussed it with Jack, another representative who chairs these meetings and who is a powerful personality. He felt detached from the issue as he had no experience of Anne's rudeness. We agreed that one course of action would be to ask for an informal discussion with the Senior Housing Officer, Sue.

At the area meeting there was a strong feeling among the
tenants that they did not want to jeopardize the good
relationship they had built up with the Housing Office over
the years. They agreed to the action I had discussed with
Jack. They nominated the fourth representative, Doris – a
respected and level-headed woman – to contact Sue and
meet her with one or two others. As usual, I took notes and
produced an informal record of the meeting.

Next day I discussed the meeting's decision with Sue, who
was clearly disturbed. She said she would observe Anne's
behaviour with tenants over the counter for a couple of
days before deciding whether to agree to the tenants'
request for a meeting. Two days later she said she saw no
basis to pursue the meeting.

Meanwhile John – who raised the complaint forcefully
but was, for justifiable reasons, absent from the tenants'
meeting – was furious that the meeting had 'pussy-footed'
around the issue. He threatened to take it up publicly when
the tenant representatives met the Housing department.

As always, I passed on a copy of the meeting's notes to
Sue. This time I did not give Anne a copy. A few days later,
in my absence, Sue read the notes and discovered I had
mentioned Anne by name. She then showed them to Anne,
who exploded. Sue reported to me that because the
complaint had been minuted, she would have to raise it with
the District Manager. He would investigate, ask the tenants
for specific allegations and, if he found them justified,
discipline Anne formally.

I can't persuade Sue that the record of the meeting was
informal and not publicly available. Anne emphatically
refuses any kind of communication with me. What, if I'd
done it differently, might have produced a more construc-
tive result?

In three weeks I leave the job. Given the short time that I
have left, what can I do towards resolving the problem?

Further Reading

The New Worker (William Temple Foundation, Manchester Business
School, Manchester M15 6PB)

The New Boss: Funding and surviving in church community work (South
Yorkshire Inner-city Community Project, Wesley House, Highfield
Place, Sheffield S2 4UR)

7

Working with Volunteers

Volunteers are our most valuable resource. They are partners with paid workers in any local piece of community work. An enormous number of clubs and organizations in this and every country are run by volunteers.

Often, when I see the long hours which are given to a piece of work and the pressures and demands people are under, it is natural to ask, why do they do it? Why do people give up their free time, often at the expense of being with family or friends, to give themselves to voluntary work?

There are also occasions when I am hit even more strongly by a contrasting question. When I see so many comfortable homes and meet people who are preoccupied with their DIY, cars, gardens and shopping, I wonder how they can live such apparently undisturbed lives when there is so much need all around them.

Volunteers offer their time and their abilities for a wide range of reasons which in themselves are a mixture of self-giving, self-interest and self-fulfilment:

- to fill time
- to repay a perceived indebtedness
- because someone they love benefits
- because someone they love is also involved
- to set an example to children
- to work as a family
- to meet people
- to please someone else
- to have fun
- to gain skills
- to gain experience
- to be visible
- to gain credit

- to express their religion or belief
- to find happiness
- to use otherwise unused gifts or skills
- because of tradition
- as part of a group
- to maintain health
- to explore new learning, ideas, etc.
- to heal (grief, personal pain, abuses, etc.)
- to avert loneliness
- because of interest
- as a hobby
- out of concern (ecology, child abuse, etc.)
- to get a tax benefit
- to balance paid work
- as an extension of a job
- because they were assigned
- to survive tragedy
- to test leadership skills
- to gain recognition
- to acquire self-confidence
- to be a change agent
- to right a wrong
- to work in a safe place
- to save money (free meals, cut down on utilities)
- to have a purpose
- to be a 'good neighbour'
- to get out of the house
- to keep active
- to experience new lifestyles
- to feel a sense of power and success.

Preparation for recruitment

One danger of working with volunteers is that we are too
informal in our recruitment. People drift into the work without a
formal interview and without our understanding fully why they
are there. In order to recruit and retain volunteers, it is
important to understand what motivates them. It has been
suggested that there are three key motivators – affiliation,
achievement and power – and once you have determined which
is the more influential in a potential volunteer, you can begin
gearing your appeals and rewards into benefits and satisfactions.

The affiliation-motivated volunteer needs a sense of belonging and
companionship, and to be liked. Working in groups works best

for them. When recruiting an affiliation-motivated person, you should:

- listen to them
- explain the team they will become part of
- comment on and praise past achievements
- tell them about personal satisfaction and social benefits they will gain
- place them in a team with lots of contact with others.

The achievement-motivated volunteer enjoys challenges and wants to do their personal best. Following a specific task to completion on their own is what they enjoy most. When recruiting an achievement-motivated person, it is best to:

- give specific tasks with specific parameters, and measure success
- provide job-related information
- give assignments that offer responsibility and advancement and the possibility of participating in decision-making
- give responsibility for an entire project and let them set their own pace and methods.

The power-motivated volunteer enjoys having impact and influence on others, but not necessarily in a negative sense. S/he can use persuasiveness to gain recognition for the organization within the community, and is a self-starter who can respond to the needs of people and keep an eye on the overall goals. They have a strong concern for reputation and status. When recruiting this type of volunteer, you could:

- present job assignments that allow increased responsibility and authority
- brief them properly about the work so that they can explain it fully to others thus gaining allies and possible new sources of funding.

The time factor

One of our greatest failings in voluntary organizations is in not telling volunteers what is expected of them and not being specific about the length of time for the work. Being open and clear about this influences the kind of person who will volunteer. There are many former volunteers who will never offer themselves again because they once took on what seemed to be a short-term piece of work and it turned out to be more like a job for life!

Short-term volunteers are not necessarily initially connected to the organization or its cause, but rather tend to volunteer with a

variety of groups – all for a limited time. They want a defined job
of short duration and are motivated by individual achievement
or professional gain. Short-term volunteers can be brought in for
specific projects or task forces with benefits experienced by the
individual and the organization.

Long-term volunteers are connected to an organization and
tend to stay for long periods of time. They are motivated by
affiliation and achievement and identify with the goals and
accomplishments of the project or piece of work. Frequently,
they grow within the organizational culture and assume positions
of authority and leadership.

What is required?

Before beginning a piece of work, or before expanding and
taking on extra volunteers or workers, it is useful to pause and
ask just what you need and how you will go about recruiting new
people. Here is a useful check-list:

- Do I know what specific tasks and responsibilities are involved
  in the job?
- Could I give prospective volunteers a clear idea of what is
  expected of them (a copy of the current job description, time
  commitment, etc.)? Remember that well-defined jobs are the
  basis of all good recruitment attempts.
- Can I identify the qualifications for the job, as well as the
  purpose and nature of the work to be done? Is there honest
  work to do?
- Does our recruitment appeal (timing, target group, type of
  media) relate to the kinds of volunteers needed?
- Have I consulted with other volunteers who will be working
  with new recruits?
- Do I have a qualified interviewer who can communicate well
  and select appropriate volunteers?
- Do I have a plan for welcoming, orienting and training
  volunteers?
- Do I have a recognition process to reward good work?

If you can answer 'yes' to all of these questions, then you not only
have the basis for an excellent recruitment effort, but you also
have a system in place to keep the new recruits.

What kind of volunteer?

In addition to working the informal structures of your community and taking advantage of all the contacts which you have, you

may need to look further afield or want to bring in some 'new blood'. This broader sweep can be facilitated by developing a recruitment plan, and through the provision of resources for its implementation. Your plan should consider the following questions:

- What is the task?
- How many volunteers do we need?
- What is the volunteer role?
- What abilities are needed?
- What training is required?
- How do we recruit?
- Who is responsible?
- What is the timetable?
- Who evaluates how we did?

Young adults

Of necessity, young people may be short-term in the present, but long-term volunteers in the future. They should be recruited by their peers, who can communicate their own experiences. Schools and colleges are including community service courses in their activities. A sense of belonging, learning good citizenship, and responsiveness to the needs of the community are all strong inducements for young people to volunteer. One study has found that respect, recognition and reward were offered as primary motivators for making volunteering more popular among teenagers. Students saw the value of experiential learning. They considered job readiness, civic contributions, increased self-esteem and social opportunities as advantages. Disadvantages included time conflicts, too much work, or fears that the experience might not be helpful to the student or the recipient.

Recruitment campaigners should include a variety of activities, combining altruism with personal growth, and contributing strong social action to alleviate human suffering.

Older volunteers

Older people command special respect in many communities and can serve as advisers and mentors for young people. They provide intergenerational communication. Older people are growing in number, providing a skilled, disciplined, educated and experienced source of volunteers.

They are a group not well-served by generalities. Some are care-givers to their grandchildren and consequently have limited time and financial resources, while for others either situational or self-imposed isolation is a deterrent to participation. The American Red Cross Society's research revealed that older people, although having been more likely to volunteer for the movement in the past, today represent those willing to give the least amount of time.

Findings relating to the development of recruitment materials for older people were that promotional materials must present this group as vital, healthy and active. They should convey opportunities for older people to meet others through volunteering, that warmth and caring are a part of volunteering, and that the activities are challenging.

Culturally diverse backgrounds

Sensitivity needs to be shown in understanding who is volunteering to work with whom, and for what reasons. People from different cultural and ethnic backgrounds will have different attitudes to volunteering – to helping and being helped. Care needs to be taken in understanding these different attitudes and in valuing them as an appropriate piece of community work is being developed for a local area.

Special populations

We are beginning to understand and value the contributions of individuals with special needs – physical, mental and emotional. Recruitment plans should include assessment for functionally involving challenged individuals. Often these plans are made in co-operation with other community organizations which have a mandate of community integration or work placement for disabled people. Ensuring the comfort of the physically disabled is essential. Transportation, access to the building and to the facilities, can make the difference between an exciting volunteer experience or an intolerable one. Disabled people contribute in many meaningful ways to the life of an organization, and their full involvement should be encouraged and facilitated.

The job description

There is an often-expressed criticism that too much formality in recruiting volunteers will be counter-productive. The soft, friendly, casual approach is the one which wins. Volunteering is about building up personal relationships and these can be subverted by too many forms and regulations. On the other hand, there is a necessary professionalism in working with volunteers which gives them a security in what they are doing and organizers a safeguard in the people who are offering themselves.

Many agencies now provide a job description for volunteers in the same way that they do for paid staff. A formal job description acts as an agreement or contract between the volunteer and the organization. It protects the rights of the volunteer as well as those of the organization. A job description for volunteers can form the basis for their training, supervision and evaluation. An added benefit is the 'self-screening' aspect which helps a potential volunteer to determine their own suitability for a piece of work. A job description should include:

- organization
- job title
- purpose of the work
- duties and responsibilities
- skills required
- special considerations (e.g. requires a vehicle)
- time requirements per week/length of assignment/training dates
- relationship: person responsible to
- benefits: training provided/certificate awarded
- reimbursement policy
- closing date for applications
- contact name for additional information and registration form.

A recruitment programme should be ongoing with an annual review and revision of the job description. Recruitment materials should be current, relevant, culturally sensitive and representative of the community at large.

When a person expresses interest in a position, a registration form can be made available and returned upon its completion. The following registration form can be adapted to meet local needs:

- name
- address
- telephone number: work and home (if applicable)
- education and special training
- place of employment
- life experience (family, work, etc.)
- special skills (e.g. languages, leadership, public speaking)
- other volunteer experience

- areas of particular interest
- availability (days/nights/hours per week)
- available transportation
- where s/he heard about the job position
- two references (not relatives)
- to be returned to:
- closing date.

Interviewing and records

An interview determines the suitability of the candidate. To protect the organization, its recipients, those who will be working with the volunteer and the volunteers themselves, it is essential that thorough screening takes place.

The interview should be conducted by an experienced, sensitive individual who understands volunteers and the organization, and who is clear about who needs what. The ability to recognize the potential of a recruit requires active listening skills. For example, the following statement:

'My church is losing members. When I volunteer for the Red Cross at the Centre, I can ask people to join' violates the principle of impartiality and is not the ideal way to recruit new volunteers to a project. Questioning a recruit about previous volunteer experience, and how satisfying the experience was, can provide clues about the candidate's suitability.

Volunteers bring rich gifts in terms of life experience. Special talents and interests which may or may not relate to the available job often can be utilized within other options. If the objective is to match the right volunteer to the right job, as opposed to merely filling the job, it will prove much more satisfactory in the long run. The purpose of interviewing is to match the volunteer to the position, to the team and to the service recipients. Volunteers need to know that they will be making a worthwhile contribution and that their skills will be used in the best possible ways. Always remain within the interviewing guidelines which you have agreed as a panel.

Once the interview is completed, the references are checked and documented. The prospective volunteer's dependability, willingness to work as a team member, and suitability are determined. Frequently, if the organization is contracted by government or a local authority to deliver a service, a criminal record search is required. The volunteer registration form, the interviewer's name, date of interview, interview outline and summary, reference documentation, and completed criminal record check, along with the placement of the volunteer, are entered in the volunteer's file.

Training volunteers

Pre-service training begins with the Volunteer Manager's first contact with the prospective volunteer. While conducting the interview, the Manager is communicating information about the organization: its mission and purpose, its structure, and the policies that affect its operation.

Adults come with expectations. Begin by finding out what those expectations are. Check for congruency with the training you are offering. It is not possible to meet all needs so be clear what can and what cannot be achieved. Set the goals of training together with the participants.

If the training model is an established one, ensure that the resource materials are current and relevant. Too often materials exist in perpetuity and consequently contain outdated research and methodology. Community workers and experienced volunteers are often willing to sit on review committees and may offer innovative suggestions for improvement. Always include experienced volunteers in the development and delivery of training events.

Methods to increase knowledge include lectures, readings, conferences, observations, interviews, panel discussions, films and videos. Place the emphasis where it is needed. Material presented in different ways emphasizes key training points. In the words of an ancient Chinese proverb:

> I hear and I forget
> I see and I remember
> I do and I understand

Methods to increase skills include role-playing, simulation situations, teaming experienced volunteers with new recruits, and on-the-job practice. Give sincere, positive reinforcement whenever possible and always relate the activity to the learning objective.

Regular participant evaluation and frequent skill competency checks reveal gaps in learning. Flexible schedules take into consideration the needs to review thoroughly and to augment knowledge as necessary.

In-service training builds on the base by providing new information and opportunity to develop teamwork. Regular monthly meetings, where volunteers can share their experiences and encourage one another; input sessions, where plans are formulated or occasions to attend seminars and conferences, ensure self-renewal and positive group motivation. Annual volunteer surveys determine strengths and weaknesses in the management cycle. It is often possible for volunteers to share in training offered by local authorities. Some can get grants to take Open University courses on community care, working with the elderly and a range of other options.

Transition training gives the experienced volunteer help in moving on to new opportunities. The volunteer may sense a need to seek fresh adventures and ask for guidance. Similarly, the supervisor or manager, sensitive to non-verbal signals from the volunteer, may initiate dialogue to clarify the volunteer's needs and wants. A tendency to keep the same volunteer delivering the same service may serve the organization while doing the individual an injustice. Supervisors and co-ordinators are advocates for volunteer potential and that advocacy may involve job enhancement or redirection.

Volunteer Training and Development

Pre-service	Orientation Training

In-service	Support Delivery Support

Transition	Support

Relationships with paid staff

Volunteer and paid staff relationships can be challenging. In poorer communities, there may be resentment over the financial gain for paid staff. In other organizations there may be too few paid staff for conflict to be an issue. But disturbing phrases – 'conflict of interest', 'volunteers block serious business', 'staff can't make demands on volunteers', 'staff treated as servants and volunteers not appreciated', 'volunteers, if not controlled, can cause problems', and 'need to make clear the difference between operations and policy' – indicate a need for greater role clarification and the development of improved communication systems.

On a more positive note, the importance of joint planning, matching the views of volunteer and paid staff, maintaining a balance of responsibility, and the keystone element – building a 'spirit of oneness' – is key to good working relationships. There are often transition tensions when volunteers move to become paid staff. Yet, volunteers and paid staff ideally become a team when each person involved is committed to the goals and activities they helped plan, carry out and evaluate.

The atmosphere in any work environment is determined by the style of leadership employed by staff, volunteers and Management Committees. In her article 'Staff/volunteer relationship "perceptions"' for the Red Cross of Canada's brochure, Gretchan E. Stringer states these relationships are based on differing perceptions of time, authority and power. From the volunteer's perspective, time is a gift. From the paid staff's perspective, time is structured and organized. The expectations placed upon a volunteer to complete a task may be unrealistic. The volunteer feels their available time is not considered. The paid staff feel the pressure to get the job done.

For the volunteer, authority is represented by the Management Committee but the first line of communication is through the Volunteer Manager, in some instances a paid staff role. The volunteer has far greater flexibility since s/he can decide to stay or leave. Staff are in a more difficult position. Hierarchical lines of authority for paid staff include the responsibilities of hiring and terminating employees. It should always be clear that volunteers do not replace or displace the work of paid staff. Volunteers enhance existing services, assist in the development of new programmes, add a community focus, and work with paid staff in a team approach.

Volunteers look to paid staff to share not only successes but also concerns. It facilitates understanding and communication if volunteers are warmly welcomed to observe or share in training sessions and learning opportunities. Communication builds good working relationships between volunteers and paid staff. A volunteer needs to feel that:

- their needs are compatible with the organization's activities
- their contribution is making a difference
- their available time and energy are considered
- they are involved in planning
- they are supported in carrying out their responsibilities
- their skills are growing
- they are part of a team
- they have a pleasant place to work

- people know them and call them by name
- their expenses are reimbursed.

Valuing volunteers

Good recognition is:

- specific
- timely
- more informal than formal
- sensitive to needs/wants
- often fun and humour-filled
- creative
- flexible.

There are many occasions, formal and informal, when the contributions of volunteers can be appreciated:

- smile and say 'thank you'
- present volunteers with awards, certificates, letters/notes of appreciation, and prizes
- listen carefully to their input and suggestions. Let them know that they do make a difference
- send appropriate greeting cards when they are ill or have a death in the family
- invite volunteers to an Annual General Meeting or a committee meeting
- promotions: give them additional responsibilities and assure them you know they can handle them
- put their picture up in your office. Have their picture taken while doing their volunteer work and give them a copy
- nominate them for local and national awards; let them know in writing of the nomination
- let them know, if they are fund-raising, how the pounds of their hard efforts are being spent
- send thank-you Christmas cards.

Remember that recruitment is an ongoing activity: 'retention' is simply the process of recruiting your volunteer every time they attend.

Evaluation of volunteer performance

Volunteers can self-evaluate their performance by means of questionnaires. Each person rates their skills and determines those areas of strength and those needing improvement. The volunteer also has an opportunity to communicate their willingness to serve in other capacities within the organization. The areas of service should also be evaluated. How does the volunteer see the programme working? What suggestions are there for improvement? And how are training, support and communications rated? Volunteer self-evaluations are most helpful in determining needs for in-service training or improvement in the work of the project.

Peer evaluation, where one volunteer is paired with another, is a non-threatening form of interpersonal evaluation. As with any assessment, a standard form should be prepared for use and the results shared only between the two volunteers, or between the volunteer and the Volunteer Manager. The volunteer must know the measurement standards being used by paid staff, have access to the results and opportunity to discuss the findings. Feedback also provides a means for assessing performance.

Clients or programme recipients/participants evaluate performance through the completion of programme evaluation forms. Any evaluation process needs to be introduced sensitively and gradually. It should not be viewed as a threatening report card but as an essential tool for improving all aspects of voluntary service. Evaluation is dealt with more fully in Chapter 10.

Terminating an agreement

Interviewing and screening, together with pre-service orientation and training, are designed with the purpose of determining the skills and appropriateness of the prospective volunteer. They provide built-in checks and balances. When a volunteer accepts a position, the individual agrees to abide by the terms and conditions of service. However, despite these cautionary measures, misplacements do occur and must be dealt with as fairly and as non-judgementally as possible.

The primary objectives of feedback are to determine ineffective aspects in the volunteer's service, to seek positive solutions and to develop a timeline for improvement. When a volunteer consciously determines to deviate from the principles, policies or procedures of the organization, it is unacceptable behaviour and can adversely affect the external profile and internal morale. If the required change in conduct is not possible, then the Volunteer Manager can request that a volunteer should leave.

Ground rules for termination interviews include:

- confidentiality
- concrete examples and explanation of unacceptable performance

- objective, non-judgemental statements to ensure the volunteer retains dignity
- allowance for ample opportunity to discuss feelings from the volunteer's perspective
- preservation of the framework of dialogue
- availability of follow-up support.

Documentation of feedback sessions where solutions and a timeline were discussed and mutually agreed to, and the request to terminate, are all held in the confidential file of the volunteer.

It is a most stressful event for both the volunteer and the Volunteer Manager. It is especially important for the Manager or Volunteer Organizer to demonstrate a sensitivity for the volunteer's feelings, which may include special factors – economic, family, health, social – in the decision. The volunteer may or may not acknowledge emotions affecting self-image. They may be reflected in frustration or anger directed towards the organization. Sometimes, a volunteer senses s/he is miscast and is looking for a 'way out'.

The Volunteer Manager also experiences mixed feelings. Self-appraisal is a natural response. Did I place the volunteer in the best place possible? Did I offer adequate support? Was the training adequate for the task? Are there alternative solutions to the situation? Have I consulted with someone who will provide me with support? Have I provided the volunteer with alternatives and support following the interview? What have I learned from this experience?

Training in terminating a volunteer is helpful when available, but it often tends to focus on liability issues for the organization rather than the emotional aspects. Role-playing the interview with a trusted colleague can build confidence for a different aspect of volunteer management.

Post-script

The classic fisherman's tale: 'The One That Got Away' . . . This lament (author unknown) was sent to a volunteer co-ordinator. You might find it interesting.

THE VOLUNTEER WHO NEVER CAME BACK

It amuses me now to think that your organization spends so much time looking for new members – when I was there all the time. Do you remember me?

I'm the lady who came to every meeting but nobody paid any attention to me. I tried several times to be friendly, but everyone seemed to have her own friends to talk to and sit with. I sat down among some unfamiliar faces several times, but they didn't pay much attention to me. I hoped someone would ask me to join one of the committees or somehow participate and contribute – but no one did.

Finally, because of illness, I missed a meeting. The next month no one asked me where I had been. I guess it didn't matter very much whether I was there or not. On the next meeting date I decided to stay home and watch a good television programme. When I attended the next meeting, no one asked me where I was the month before.

You might say that I'm a good person, I have a good family, and love my community. You know who else I am? I'm the member who never came back.

8

Effective Meetings and Groups

Working with people in groups and conducting meetings are essential features of any piece of community work. For any meeting or group to work well and be effective, planning is the essential ingredient. After many successful meetings or groups, when things have gone smoothly and everyone feels satisfied, it will be said 'We did that well' or 'Wasn't it surprising that we were able to tackle that complicated subject so well?' Of course, it is only surprising to those who are not very aware of what is going on in a meeting. To the perceptive and skilled, or to those who have been able to learn through experience, a successful meeting or group is one which has been planned well and has had as much preparation put into it as possible.

As well as good planning before a meeting, people need to feel that, as discussion takes place, they are working within a secure framework and that they will be allowed a fair hearing. They need to know why they are there, to feel they have been able to participate in discussions, to feel that they can go along with a decision they do not fully agree with because they have been heard, that they can commit themselves to what has been decided, and that they know what action is required of them after a meeting. It is also a great help if they can rely on getting a fairly accurate record, or set of minutes, reasonably soon after the meeting.

Types of meetings

Public meetings These can be large in numbers and are often occasions when a major speaker will give an address from the front of a hall, and when people can speak openly from the body of the meeting.

Committee meetings An element of formality is evident. There will be a chairperson who will steer people through an agenda.

Minutes will be taken by a secretary and circulated to all those present. The members of a committee will often have been elected or appointed by the public or by another group.

Discussion groups Informality is more a characteristic of these events, even though they will need to be planned. Discussion groups are designed to allow more free-ranging contributions. They often take place in homes or smaller rooms and may exist to explore a particular subject, to encourage the exchange of opinions and to provide an atmosphere in which people can grow and develop. It is not necessary that conclusions should be reached, and votes are unlikely to be taken.

This chapter will have two sections: one will look at the planning and conduct of formal meetings or committees, the other will look at informal discussion groups.

Formal meetings

Formal meetings, the duties of an officer and the legal require-ments of Trustees are dealt with in Chapter 4. What follows is designed to help put those requirements into practice.

Why are people there?

Although some sceptics may doubt it, all committees exist for a reason. Similarly the members of a committee need to know why they are there and what the purpose of the committee is.

A committee will have a task. This is likely to be concerned with the management of a project. At the 'highest' level it will be a Committee of Trustees who have the legal responsibility for the direction of a project and its financial management. Trustees are nominated or appointed and will be names in a legal document. Management Committees will have a wider variety of people on them, according to their special experience and expertise. They, like meetings of Trustees, will probably have members of staff in attendance. Subcommittees will have been set up for an even more specific task. They may have a shorter life and will need to report regularly to a Management Committee. They work best if they are made up of a small number of people.

In each case, if the purpose of a committee is clear then it will be easier to recruit members, to keep their commitment, and to know the limits of accountability when decisions are being made.

Frequency of meetings

The number of times a committee should meet needs to be directly related to its task. I was once invited to advise the 98th meeting in three years of a church growth group which had yet to put its proposals to the Church Council! Trustees will meet infrequently, probably two or three times a year. Management Committees will need to meet every two months or so, and Subcommittees more frequently, but for a limited length of time.

Length of service

People may well be more willing to join a committee if they know that they are not committing themselves to a 'life sentence'. Some constitutions now state the length of time a member can serve, and if that term is renewable. Where this provision does not exist, it is often helpful to agree 'working practice' so that a committee has a rotation with, say, one-third of its members retiring every one or two years.

Framing an agenda

The more there is consultation in putting an agenda together the more likely it is that people will be committed to it and that they will be prepared to enter into a full discussion. The biggest possible disaster is for a chairperson to think that they alone know what needs to be discussed and that everyone else will fall into line. Some organizations keep a diary and ask that, before a certain date, anyone who wants business included should make their bid, putting alongside their entry an estimate of the time needed for discussion. If the committee is a large one then perhaps the officers or Standing Committee will meet to decide on an agenda.

It is sometimes thought over-scrupulous to put timings on an agenda. Whether or not everyone has timings, the Chair should always have a clear idea about how long each agenda item might take. It is often helpful to state, either on the agenda or at the beginning of a meeting, which are the main items for discussion. Otherwise large amounts of time may be taken up with relatively minor items early on the agenda and not enough time will be left for adequate discussion of major items later on in the meeting.

With the formal notice of a meeting will go the final agenda. Each item should be clear enough for members of the committee to be able at least to understand what the subject is. Committee members will find it much easier to come to an informal decision if they have as much appropriate information as possible. This may be in the form of background papers or it may be that someone other than the Chair is asked to prepare and introduce a subject. If there are briefing or background papers these should be enclosed and marked in some way on the agenda.

Agenda format

It can be helpful to use a consistent agenda format, for example:

1. Apologies, welcome and agenda review
2. Minutes of last meeting
3. Matters arising not covered elsewhere on the agenda
4. Internal committee matters (new committee members, etc.)
5. Financial report
6. Funding and fund-raising
7. Staff matters
8. Activities or issues specific to this organization of meeting
9. Training
10. Future meetings (including Chair and minute-taker for next meeting, if it rotates)
11. Any other business.

An agenda like this tells participants broadly what topics will be covered, but does not give any idea of the specific items for the meeting. Agendas are far more useful if, under each main heading, items to be dealt with are detailed, for example:

After-school and holiday activities
(a) After-school club
(b) Craft group
(c) Swimming club
(d) Easter playscheme.

This makes it clearer what will be on the agenda, but participants still do not know why anything is there: for information, discussion, consultation, decision or review. Meetings are far easier to chair and participate in if the 'why' is added, and if the agenda also indicates who will introduce the item:

After-school and holiday activities
(a) After-school club: report on current and future activities (Sarah)
(b) Craft group: report (Sarah)
(c) Swimming club: report on difficulties with Eastway Pool (Ali). Decision required on response to Eastway
(d) Easter playscheme: initial proposals from staff (Narinder). Committee is asked to discuss these, make further proposals and decide priorities.

The time and place

Often, unwittingly, meetings take place at times when some people cannot attend. This cannot always be checked out by

asking the people who do attend a meeting – obviously it is
convenient for them! One way of getting the time for a meeting
right – and there is never an absolutely right time – is to look at
the purpose of a committee, at the kind of people you want to join
it, and then to ask what time in the day they are most likely to be
available. Meetings which span the time when children are to be
collected from school preclude some parents. A meeting beginning at 5.00 or 5.30 or 6.00pm will make all the difference to
many working people. If an end-time is given for a meeting it is
important that it is kept, or that an extension is negotiated with
the whole meeting.

The setting for a meeting can have a crucial effect on its
atmosphere and consequently on how decisions are made.
Thought needs to be given about whether chairs are set out in
rows, or in a semi-circle or circle. Sometimes people will be able to
handle their papers better if they are sitting at a table – round or
square? Less formal committees may sit around in armchairs and
meet in homes. One of the most important features is that,
whatever the room, it should be free of interruptions, from
telephones ringing or people 'just looking in'.

Chairing a meeting

Chairpeople come in all shapes and sizes. Sometimes they are
among the most experienced people in a committee, sometimes
they will have little or no experience of ever chairing a meeting
before. Occasionally a chairperson will have experience of
chairing other kinds of meetings, with their own constitutions
and traditions – a Board of Directors, a Trade Union meeting, a
local authority committee. These experiences are not always
helpful. The more a chairperson is aware of their own strengths
and weaknesses, the more likely they are to be able to help a
committee function harmoniously and efficiently.

The kinds of statements a chairperson makes or the questions
asked are important. It requires more courage, tact and verbal
skill to express a different point of view when the Chair opens the
proceedings with 'I think we are all agreed that the way forward
is so and so', than when the Chair says 'Can we discuss what we
feel to be the best way forward?' The first statement can either
inhibit discussion and drive feelings underground, or generate
conflict and faction. The second can stimulate open and objective
discussion.

How and when the Chair provides information or submits
their own ideas is also important. To get the best out of a
committee it is necessary to put in all the relevant information in

such a way that the members can understand and handle it. Partial or slanted information can prevent the committee from seeing the real facts. Similarly, if the potential of the committee is to be realized, the Chair may have to hold back ideas until others have had a chance to put theirs. It is much better to work for an atmosphere and attitudes where all ideas are looked at on merit and not in relation to who suggested them in the first place.

Your part as a committee member

You can participate most effectively if you give yourself the following guidelines:

- Learn about the issues being discussed. Read minutes from previous meetings and papers circulated for the coming meeting. Talk to people.
- Listen to other people during the meeting. Pick up on what they are saying, instead of constantly thinking of your rejoinder, or barging in with your own ideas or opinion.
- Think before you open your mouth. If necessary, make notes of what you want to say.
- Speak clearly and to the point. Be assertive (clear about what you want to say) without being obnoxious, aggressive or manipulative.

- Do not be afraid to speak. The worst that can happen is that you will be made to feel silly or stupid by ignorant, rude people. The best is that others who have less confidence than you will welcome your speaking up and gain confidence and strength from your comments.
- Be reasonable. Despite what you think, yours is not the only valid point of view. Do not put people down, try to score points or throw tantrums. Treat other people as you would like to be treated. Let them have their say, even if they are criticizing or misunderstanding you, without constantly interrupting. Make notes of the points you want to come back to.
- Let go. Even if you are 100 per cent sure the group is making a wrong decision, in the end you may have to let them do it. Everyone makes mistakes, and hopefully the group will learn from theirs.

Reaching a decision

Coming to a decision at a meeting is in some part linked with the problem of time. Some committees' time is spent in going over the same ground again and again, without seeming to get any further forward. What can the Chair do about this?

- Recognize the issues that need to be aired thoroughly before people are ready to come to a decision; some people, by nature, seem to need longer to mull over things than others. The application of a 'guillotine' or even to hasten unduly the process may cause unfavourable repercussions at a later date. If the Chair feels that the issue under discussion is of this sort, it may be that asking the question, 'Would you like to make a decision tonight, or would you prefer to defer a decision until we have more information or have had time to think and talk about it?' would help the committee to progress.
- Make sure that the issues which are being discussed are clear to the committee members. One way in which this can be done is by ensuring that all relevant information is available for the meeting in an intelligible form. The Chair can also ask questions which may encourage people to indicate when they don't understand something. Sometimes it can be helpful to ask a question for more information, sometimes restate or rephrase a point which has just been made.
- Summarize and recapitulate the points which have been made during the course of the discussion. One way of doing this is to itemize them on a flip-chart. This serves as a

reminder of what has been said and the progress made, and helps people to feel that the points they have made during the course of the discussion are receiving due attention. Therefore they do not need to repeat them over and over again.

- Ask questions which remind the committee of the task in hand: 'Are you ready to vote?' or 'Do you wish to pursue this further?'
- When the discussion goes off at a tangent, as often it does, the Chair can remind people of the subject, summarize where the discussion has got to, ask people for agreement, and for permission to move on.

Implementing decisions

Sometimes it is such a relief that, after a long and difficult discussion, any decision can be reached at all. What is forgotten is the need to agree who will carry out a decision. The familiar questions – what?, how?, who?, when? – can help to focus responsibility and lead to action.

- What has been decided? Is the decision clear? Does everyone understand what has been decided? Does a decision have real agreement? – silence frequently does not mean consent.
- How will a decision be implemented? Are there sufficient resources? Has a realistic decision been made? – can what has been decided actually be done? Is there a budget? How much can be spent? Can other people be brought in to help?
- Who is going to implement a decision? Has anyone agreed to take responsibility? Are their names in the minutes? Were they at the meeting? If not, who will brief them?
- By when will a decision be carried out? Is there a stated timescale for the task? Is it written down? Will a person or group be expected to report back, and by when?
- Who will check it out? Is the Chair also the progress-chaser? Who has the responsibility for making sure that work is done between meetings?

Notes or minutes

It is very important to keep a record of the briefest of meetings. It was Sir Humphrey, the powerful civil servant in *Yes Minister*, who said that it does not really matter what is said in a meeting, the important thing is for the minutes to say things in the way that the Civil Service wants! This may be a travesty of the truth but it does emphasize how important the Secretary or minute-taker is. As a general rule, the more formal the meeting, the more formal the minutes. They do always need to be given headings, often the ones which relate to the title of the item on the agenda. Often paragraphs are numbered and sub-divided for easy reference.

Effective committees are one which not only make decisions but which also decide who is going to carry out, or act on, a decision; by when, and how they will report back. Working minutes often have an 'Action' column along one side with names in it, so that everyone knows who should be doing what and so that progress-chasing can be carried out if necessary. For ease of communication, and so that everyone can be reminded of who should be doing what, it is helpful if minutes can be circulated within two weeks of a meeting taking place.

Conclusion

We end where we began. Effective meetings are the result of good planning and preparation. People perform best if they can have freedom of expression within a secure framework. Decisions can be carried out most effectively if they are clear and if it is understood by all who is to do what and by when.

Effective groups

A discussion group is not a committee and it will fail in its effectiveness if its leaders behave like chairpeople and if its members behave like committee sitters. A discussion group has a much greater degree of informality and exists for a different purpose. However, in one area a discussion group is exactly the same as a committee: it will work best if it is carefully planned and adequately structured.

The range of informal groups in community projects and community development work is very wide indeed. People will sit around in the corner of a hall or in a coffee lounge and discuss an issue in great depth. A community centre or a church may advertise a series of discussions on a chosen subject and hope that people will turn up. In a more organized way, it may be the development policy of an organization or a church to have groups meeting in centres and people's homes for a fixed period, all discussing the same topic. In another situation there may be a pressing, local, social topic and a community worker may organize a series of evenings or a one-day consultation to explore a subject. As varied as these examples are, each discussion group relies on informality for its effectiveness.

Forming a group

On the surface there is a real and very genuine reason why some people join groups: they want to understand more about a subject for themselves. Other people will know that there is a pressing local problem and they will join a discussion group to hear more about it and to see how they can co-operate with others. Some people will join a group so that they can gain greater commitment to an organization and begin to understand more about the beliefs and values of other members. In every group there is also an element that people are there because they value the company, the social integration; they want a night out and they need to make friends.

Group leaders will need to be aware that things are happening at different levels within the life and activities of a group. They will also need to be aware of their own motives in convening a group. These may not be very complimentary reasons, like the need to feel that something tangible can be shown for their work. More optimistically, many workers will hope that, through the experience of work in a group, group members will grow and develop in their personal lives, and will gain a heightened awareness of social and political concerns.

The structuring of informal groups that I shall be describing is that where people meet to consider a subject, rather than for primarily social purposes. I shall not be describing therapy groups, where the primary reason for attending would be to address personal questions or the problems of those present.

Let us imagine that the National Council for Refugees has produced a six-session study pack on the question of refugees in the Middle East. There is a considerable local population who are themselves either refugees or are the descendants of refugees.

You hope that, by organizing a series of group discussions, you may inform local people of an international problem and at the same time encourage them to share experiences of being refugees and of having to settle in a new country. In addition, you hope that those whose families have lived in this country for many generations will also come and hear the problems of recent arrivals. From past experience, you expect a group of ten, not all of whom will come every week. You begin to plan how the course of discussions will be organized and led.

Co-leadership

It is always best to 'lead' the group together with another person. Two people make better plans, two people can observe different things taking place in a group, and partners can interrupt or intervene when the other gets stuck or cannot see what is happening. Co-leadership also means that different styles can be used and that a wider range of experience is brought into the life of a group.

'Lead' is a misleading word in the life of a small group. Other words are coming into use which describe what needs to happen if a group is to have a good life. One most appropriate word is 'facilitate', since it suggests not leadership but the ability to work in a way that will allow others to contribute their own wisdom and opinions.

Group leadership, co-leadership or facilitation is not about convening a group, providing a series of talks about a particular subject and then allowing, or rather hoping, that there will be some small discussion after; and, of course, that no one will dominate! It is interested in creating, or designing, a framework which will allow and enable discussion to take place. Such leadership is more concerned with encouraging and guiding discussion than it is with presenting facts or giving 'introductory talks'.

Choice and preparation of a subject

We have already looked at an example of how the subject of being a stranger or refugee might fit one particular neighbourhood. Organizers should be sensitive to the needs of a local area in their choice of subject. Equally, they may make a deliberate choice of a subject where they feel issues need to be raised and brought in to a local agenda.

Occasionally 'off the shelf' courses might be appropriate. More frequently, experienced group leaders will decide upon a subject and then look around at a range of materials which might be used for different sessions. Selection of resource material will be much more time-consuming, but it will fit much more appropriately the needs of a particular local group.

Venue

The choice of the right room for a discussion is extremely important. A room which is too long and thin, or which has awkward corners, will make it hard for people to see one another. Here is a check-list of other things to try and get right.

- Will refreshments be at the beginning, in the middle or at the end of a discussion?
- Can the chairs be arranged in a kind of circle? Three people on a sofa make a straight line. Pack it with cushions so that there is only room for two.
- Make sure the telephone is unplugged or can be answered in another room.
- Decide who will answer the door to late-comers and how they will be briefed.
- If a projector, tape recorder or video is to be used, get it set up before the meeting begins.
- Will you need a flip-chart?
- Have you got enough different coloured felt pens if people are expected to draw things?

Time and frequency of meetings

The time of a meeting and its day in the week will, inevitably, exclude some people. It is important to canvass the potential constituency as thoroughly as possible so that you avoid obvious mistakes or clashes with any other regular meetings. Timings should be clear, endings as well as beginnings.

If you are using a room in a hall or community centre, check to see if there is a noisy activity taking place in another room which is likely to disturb you. Sticking to the same meeting place is usually best unless you have a good reason for circulating. Nothing is more frustrating than the confusion of 'Where is the meeting this week?'

Meetings which appear to be infrequent lose the commitment of members. 'Every Thursday at 8.00' or some other memorable peg is useful to get people there. Occasionally people prefer fortnightly meetings or 'on the third Tuesday of the month'. A printed programme with all the details is a great help.

Designing a discussion

Some people shy away from the idea of 'designing' the way in which a discussion can be constructed. They suspect manipulation. Designing a discussion means constructing a framework in which people will be able to gain information and exchange opinions in the easiest possible way.

Our refugee discussion pack is in six sessions. Each has a title and a main theme, and there is factual material and questions for discussion. The leaders or facilitators can divide the discussion time into a series of sections. They might look like this:

8.00	Introductions
8.10	Introduction of the material
8.20	General discussion
8.35	Break into threes for special questions
8.50	Share ideas
9.00	Coffee break
9.15	Introduction of second topic
9.20	Second discussion
9.40	Conclusions
9.50	Work between meetings, plan for next discussion.

This may seem too structured. Another kind of plan would be for the leaders to make an introduction and then to have a series of questions which they introduce at intervals to develop the discussion. Before they introduce a new aspect they will summarize the discussion so far. I call this sequence launch–guide–summarize. A design for an evening might look like the illustration opposite.

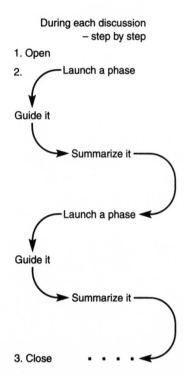

During each discussion
– step by step

1. Open
2.   Launch a phase

Guide it

              Summarize it

              Launch a phase

Guide it

              Summarize it

3. Close   ▪ ▪ ▪ ▪

Ice-breakers and introductions

At the beginning of the first meeting it is important to do rather more than just going round the circle getting everyone to give their names. The use of one or two 'ice-breaker' exercises will help everyone to get to know one another and will set the participative style for the rest of the discussion. Here are some easy-to-use introductory exercises:

1. Get the group to split into pairs and allow two minutes each for members to introduce themselves to each other. Then in the full group each person introduces their partner. More than anything else, this is an exercise in listening. There may be questions to and fro in the group for clarification or further information.
2. Photocopy the road signs on p. 130 and give them out to each member of the group. Get them to identify two signs which represent good things about the subject and two signs which represent difficult things. Ask them to share their signs in pairs, and then with the rest of the group.

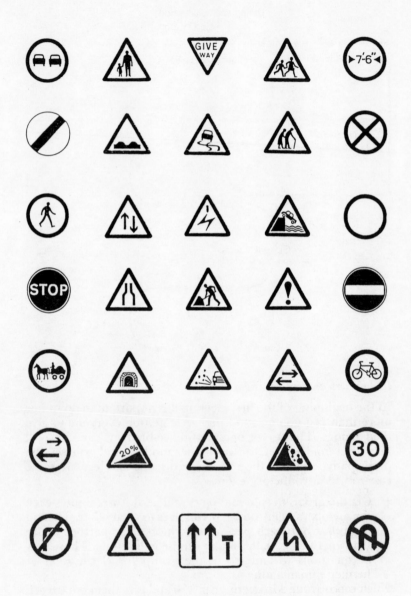

3. Give everyone a sheet of paper divided into quarters. Get them to fill the sections in, with headings such as these:

My favourite meal	What I would really like to be called
Where I would like to be if I were not here	The person I most admire is . . . .

Each member then reads out their answers to the whole group.

4. Everyone has a piece of paper with a shield drawn on it:

They fill it with their 'family coat of arms'. This can be one full picture, or a shield divided into halves, quarters or whatever. Such an idea takes some time and it may be best done between meetings and presented the next time.

5. Get people to look at the figures on and around the tree printed on p. 132. Ask them to try to identify themselves in relation to the subject being discussed. This exercise might be used again at the end of the course for evaluation.

There are many other 'ice-breaker' introduction exercises which can be found in group leadership books, or which can be invented by hosts. Experience shows that it is best to allow plenty of time for people's explanations in each exercise. For some it will be a new and important experience, being listened to in such a patient and absorbing way. The whole group will discover the

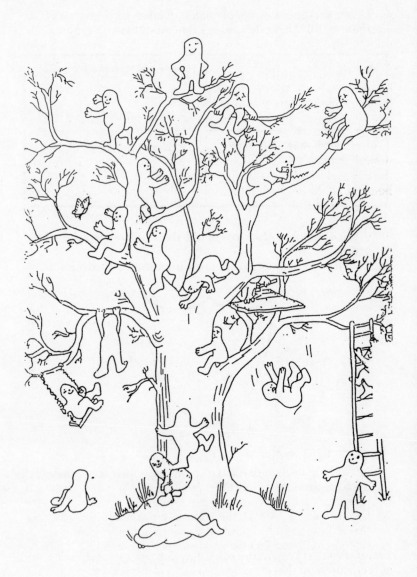

importance of listening and trying to understand the 'story' or 'journey so far' of each of the other members. Introductions done in this sympathetic and patient way will set the scene and the style of the sharing and mutual learning which is to come.

Another helpful thing about such exercises is that everyone, but especially the leaders, will get to know from a person's background and circumstances why they are expressing certain opinions. It will also help to promote sensitivity when introducing some further subjects, avoiding inappropriate ways.

The group will also be helped with elementary things like timing. If John has said he is rushing straight from work, you will understand why he is sometimes late. If Mary says she cannot get home at 10.00 pm without a lift, and that her husband is always waiting for her, then you must end on time. You will, of course, share very much more and such exercises will contribute to building up an atmosphere of mutual trust and support.

Maintaining the life of a group

Group leaders should try to be aware of keeping a balance of what is happening in the life of a group. The method for observation was first suggested by Dr John Adair and consists of three interlocking circles.

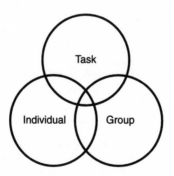

Task It is vital to keep to the subject of the evening, unless there is agreement by all that a change can be made. It is the easiest thing in the world to be diverted by someone's 'hobby-horse' or by some unconnected new idea which someone might have.

Individual Sensitive leaders will be careful to see who is taking part in the discussion and who is not. Sometimes people will want to be left alone to listen. On other occasions, especially if the 'welcome' sessions have gone well, leaders will try to find ways of drawing quiet people in.

It is sometimes helpful to keep a 'spider's web' of how the discussion is going, drawing connecting lines on a note pad as the session develops:

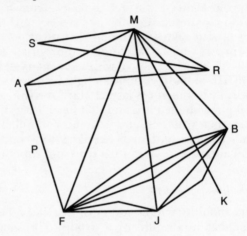

M is hogging things. F, B and J like talking to each other. P is left out. Could anything be done?

Group If things go well, the group will develop strong bonds among its members. This 'natural' strength may well be the result of hard work by the leaders to draw everyone in and keep a balance in the conversation. As new subjects crop up, it is important to allow all group members to make a contribution and to feel that they are really of interest to all the others.

Ending a group

One way to encourage people to join a group is to make it clear that meetings are not going to go on for ever. It is very helpful to say that this is a six- or eight-week series and that, if there is to be any continuation, there will be a break of several weeks before beginning again.

Most people who have shared in the life of a small group will have valued the experience. They will have found it a positive thing to contribute their own opinions and to know that others have listened and taken them seriously. Those who are committed to participative community development methods will know that the encouragement of support and discussion in small groups is a vital element in the 'success' of any piece of work.

CASE STUDY
Non-learning in large groups

I am a member of a Joint Committee, comprising representatives from two Methodist Circuits, which organized an
afternoon consultation on 'Racism in the Church'. We
agreed to invite a member of the local Community Relations Council to be the Speaker and to guide our thinking.
She had been recommended by one of the committee
members. She accepted our invitation. We set up a sub-
group to plan this event.

The Speaker requested six group leaders and these were
chosen from amongst the churches. She met them prior to
the event to explain the structure she proposed for the
afternoon and to brief them on what they would be
required to do to facilitate the consultation.

At the consultation (attended by 65 people) I was a
participating member with no authority. The Speaker was
introduced by one of my colleagues, who chaired the
opening sessions. The Speaker explained to the consultation that she had primed the group workers to guide six
groups. Each would examine one of four issues concerning
racism. These were:

- experiencing the effects of oppression (two groups)
- the process of institutionalized racism (two groups)
- a choice between integration, multi-cultural or
  anti-racism
- racism in education.

We were arbitrarily divided into six groups and told to go
off and spend some time discussing the issues. We would
then return and share our findings.

My group was asked by our group leader to identify
occasions when we had felt oppressed. A discussion ensued
as to the meaning of oppression and the little likelihood of
any of white, middle-class Christians ever having experienced it. This went on for about five minutes until the
group worker explained that the purpose of the exercise
was to try to identify with the feelings of the oppressed.
More out of empathy for the worker than out of sympathy
for the task, I suggested that we could accept that there was
a vast difference of degree but that we might be able to

identify incidents in which we had felt oppressed. After a pause for thought we were asked to share our findings with our neighbours.

Finally we were invited to compare what we had done about being oppressed when we had experienced it, and what we might do now if it were to re-occur. This led to further expressions of dissatisfaction with the lack of input into the consultation, the waste of busy people's time, and the somewhat contrived tasks given to our group. All this took about an hour, after which we were recalled to the plenary session.

Each group had been given a sheet of paper on which to record its findings. Three of the six groups used it; two of the reporters also spoke of the paper at great length.

In the course of a report on 'Racism in Education' the group was represented as deciding that on the evidence it could not be concluded that racial discrimination existed in educational opportunities in our area. A member of the consultation, unable to contain himself any longer, leapt to his feet exclaiming 'I just do not believe what I am hearing; how much more evidence do you need?' Whereupon the Chairman jumped to his feet and shouted across the meeting 'We are simply at the reporting back stage – kindly sit down and allow it to continue!'

After a further two or three minutes the Speaker invited general questions or comments. I took the opportunity to share my surprise about the findings of the group looking at racism in education, and asked what further evidence they needed before coming to this conclusion. We then discovered that the group had been fed statistical information by the group leader, on the basis of which no firm conclusion could be reached. Individually and collectively they recognized the presence of racism in education, but they had been led to believe that their task was only to comment upon the evidence before them.

The Speaker then summed up by saying that she was sure that we would agree that it was good to talk about this subject, that we would all have learnt something, and please look round the exhibition material which would remain on display until after the service following the tea.

After the consultation I sensed that other people were as frustrated as I was over the wasted opportunity on the part of an 'expert' to advance my understanding of racism. My fear is that the only thing that most people may have learnt is not to waste time on another Sunday afternoon when the

Joint Committee organizes a further consultation on this or any other subject!

CASE STUDY
The compulsive volunteer

I work in a diocesan job with handicapped people and their families. Initially, one of my responsibilities was supporting the volunteers who worked at parish level with these families. As the number of volunteers grew I felt that, in order to be more effective in my support, I should gather them into small local groups, based on deaneries.

Invitations were sent out and three groups were formed, each with eight to ten members. At the first meeting, I agreed to act as co-ordinator in two of the groups for the first year. After that the groups were to choose a new co-ordinator from amongst themselves. (My colleague did the same with the third group.)

For the first year these groups met every two months. They all emerged with objectives which were amazingly similar, so a small paper was prepared stating these and suggested ways to meet them. Speakers were invited to help them develop their skills and forge links with other specialist organizations, evenings of prayer were arranged and the groups began to bond together.

Throughout the year I gradually prepared the groups for autonomy by helping them to accept responsibilities within the group. I hoped in this way that when the time came for me to withdraw, the co-ordinator wouldn't have any added extras and the group would be working together.

One group gave me cause for concern. John (who had numerous other commitments in the parish) was always volunteering to undertake the various responsibilities within the group. I had managed during the year to steer many of these to other group members; the ones he had undertaken were either half-completed or forgotten about.

As the time for my withdrawal from the group drew nearer, I became more and more worried that John would be the one the group chose as co-ordinator. I felt sure that if that happened the group wouldn't function efficiently for much longer.

On the evening planned for changing co-ordinators we began by discussing this role, and the amount of time needed to do the work well. We had a fairly good discussion and after coffee I asked for nominations from the group. John was nominated (or rather, he half-nominated himself) and was backed by several members. I asked him if he could cope with the extra work involved with all his other commitments. He was quite sure he could! There were no other nominations as everyone agreed he was the right person. I felt powerless to do anything but accept the group decision.

After the meeting closed I talked to John again about his role, gave him my file and volunteered any help he might need in preparing for the next meeting. The offer wasn't taken up. The next and two subsequent meetings were chaotic, and attendance diminished. One could sense a feeling of dissatisfaction amongst the group but no one seemed to be able to say anything to John.

How could I have avoided this situation? what can I do now?

Further Reading

Taking the Chair at Meetings (The Methodist Church and Avec)
Team Spirit, Dr David Cormack (MARC, 1987)
Group Meetings That Work, Catherine Widdicombe (St Paul Press, 1994)
Learning for Life: A handbook of adult religious education, Yvonne Craig (Mowbray, 1994)

9

Beliefs, Values and the Churches

Beliefs behind the actions

I am frequently surprised when running courses and consultations on church and community work, by the range of approaches that Christians bring to their work. Some come searching for a Christian or 'theological' justification for their work, as if they needed to find explanations, after the event, to underpin the community work that they have been doing. At the other extreme there are many, probably more, who will only bring mention of their beliefs into a course if prompted to do so by some particular exercise that I am offering. They are content to let their actions be explained by a need that they have seen and to which they have responded. If there is no conflict with their beliefs then there is no need for a public display of motives or an examination of underlying assumptions.

Christianity is mentioned most often when workers come into conflict with a church either because there is a difference of aim over a piece of work, or because there is a problem over employment or the way in which employees or volunteers are being treated.

Community-minded churches

I use a term like 'community-minded' to describe particular kinds of congregations. They can belong to almost any denomination. These churches do not have high boundaries or barriers between those who are members and those who are not. They blend almost too easily into their local community. Church buildings will be used for a range of community activities and there will be little anxiety about whether users are ever likely 'to come to church'.

Church members will be equally at home in activities which are not sponsored by their church. It will be enough to know that they are working with others to provide community care in an appropriate way.

Membership churches

Congregations which are defined by their adherents joining and becoming members, associating themselves with a particular set of beliefs, have more difficulty in engaging in unconditional community work. If church membership is about cultivating a particular set of beliefs and in persuading others to come and join, then community work which makes no demands, and which involves co-operating with those who have different beliefs, can pose a problem. Community care can be understood but community development work and certainly broad-based organizing pose problems.

Membership churches are the ones which are growing and which do not have as many financial problems. They are encountering new problems, however, as they become more settled into their local communities. One worker who came to me described her local situation which was very typical of such churches.

The local evangelical church had flourished and had a number of pensioners as members. It began an informal club one day a week. Because it went so well it opened on another day and a worker was employed. People began to ask if they could bring their friends. The same church had parents with young children. A mother and toddler group was begun on one morning a week. Two workers were employed. These mothers also wanted to bring their friends and later, when their children went to school, wanted the facility to stay open for other lonely parents in the community. A co-ordinator was employed to oversee all the church community work.

Now, some of the church members were questioning the purpose of all these activities and the use of the money. Was the church for believers and was their work for overt evangelism, or were they now happy to offer community facilities with no strings or faith demands?

A biblical basis for community work

One of the best known of Jesus' parables, prompting people to care for others, is that of the Good Samaritan. In it a man is attacked by robbers on the road from Jerusalem to Jericho. Whether for personal reasons or for those to do with ritual purity we do not know, but a priest and a Levite pass him by. The injured man is helped by an outsider, a Samaritan, who takes him to an inn and pays for his welfare. From this graphic and somewhat guilt-inducing story, which is told by Jesus in answer to the question 'Who is my neighbour?' there is seen the general reinforcement of the obligation on any Christian to be active in the care and welfare of those in need.

In his book *On the Edge of the Primeval Forest*, Dr Albert Schweitzer tells that he was prompted to spend the rest of his lifetime working in Africa by the impact on him of the story of Dives and Lazarus (Luke 16.19–31). A rich man and a poor man are contrasted in this life and then, at the time of judgement, the rich man is condemned for not acting on stories and commands about the care for the poor while he had the opportunity in this life. The story continues to move many people to greater social action – both to be offended by the gap between rich and poor, and to try to do something about it.

The Old Testament is a history of a people moving from itinerant herdsmen to a settled people with towns and cities, judges and then kings. Its books tell stories of warfare and the conquering of people from alien tribes. We read twice the story of exile and return. Within narratives of warfare and considerable bloodshed there emerge other consistent themes from judges, kings, prophets and poets. These themes are about the establishment of peace and justice, about the use and abuse of power, and about the rights of individuals in the face of injustice and exploitation.

So, within the strands of community work, Christians and almost all others with similar concerns will look towards the establishment of the kind of society which is hoped for, and in many cases legislated for, in the Old Testament. It is also seen in the way in which Jesus lived and in the things which he taught. Care for individuals and groups in society is probably best summed up for very many Christians involved in care and community work by the story from St Matthew's gospel about the Kingdom and about judgement (Matthew 25.31–46).

Theological implications for Christians

There is a frequently quoted response of Dom Helder Camara about his work in South America: 'When I feed the hungry they call me a saint. When I ask why people are hungry they call me a communist.' Christians live with the same kind of tension. In societies where the gap between rich and poor is becoming greater it is difficult, and probably insensitive, to work in community care or community development and not begin to ask questions about why things are as they are, and to look beyond the immediate need to its causes. Such thoughts are, of course, disturbing, but they do not necessarily mean that workers and church members will go out and join a political party to try and put things right. What has happened is that people involved in community work have begun to ask themselves questions about the situations they are involved with, they have tried to see why they are offended by the conditions in which many people have to live, and they have looked at the sources of their beliefs in the scriptures and in Christian tradition. This kind of thinking and re-evaluation has come to be called 'reflection' or 'theological reflection' or 'reflecting an experience'.

This process of thinking has now become very systematic and developed in some areas of church life. The original method of reflection which has been the source of thought and practice for many people has its origins in the work and writings of the South American educationalist and Liberation Theology worker Paulo Freire. He has suggested a cycle of action–reflection for us all, but particularly for those involved in community work and community education.

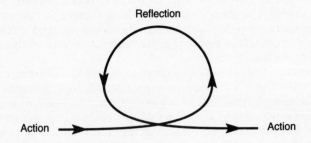

Very basically, Freire suggests that learning for most people takes place through activity rather than in the classroom and through lectures. Parents learn about community action by lobbying to get a pedestrian crossing near their school. Freire says that the experience of learning is understood when time is taken from activity to ask 'What did we do there, what lessons have we learned, what should we do or what do we need to be more effective next time?' This basic sitting down and looking at the experience of learning through activity is, for Freire and for very many of those he has influenced, a fundamental method for people and communities to understand their learning.

In Christian communities this way of working has been developed or extended to bring in beliefs and a strategy for further action. The report *Faith in Leeds* published in 1986 described a Pastoral Circle.

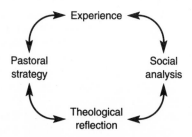

What this cycle describes is the movement from the experience gained in a piece of work to the context in which it was done. Then come questions and values which arise from an understanding of the scriptures and the values of the Christian tradition. There is some debate about whether values should come at the beginning of a piece of 'Christian' work, but the general opinion of those involved in community work is that theological reflection is as much about asking questions as it is about providing answers. If this is the case then it is appropriate for the theological reflection to come at this stage.

Pastoral strategy asks that a local piece of work be seen within a much wider context of the work either of the province, district or diocese or within the strategy of a Council of Churches or a local congregation. It is probably true to say that a piece of community work is more likely to inform and motivate pastoral strategy than receive direction from it. The cycle then continues with further work and action which hopefully is more effective, both locally and within community and church structures, as a result of this process of reflection.

To think and work in this way can have an exhilarating and a disturbing effect on volunteers, staff and managers in a project. The horizons of faith will have been broadened and the ways in which the Christian faith can bring searching questions to a piece of work will perhaps be experienced for the first time.

Christian hope and community work

Many of those involved in community work think and act with their attention on the future. They speak about people and communities reaching their full potential. Joe Hasler, in his booklet *Becoming Human Together*, published by the diocese of Bristol, describes local stories and 'gossip' as vehicles which contain the power of hope for local communities. He says 'I use the word "myth" deliberately because the stories people tell often contain the story of the struggle between right and wrong, hope and despair, life and death, tragedy and triumph, and other great mythological themes. Such myths are often "written" large in the oral traditions of local communities. Hope, then, is a basic concern for community workers.' Hasler looks to the concept of hope for his connection with the Christian faith. He uses the writings of Jürgen Moltmann, one of whose books is called *A Theology of Hope* (SCM, 1967).

The argument developed is that creation is accepted as it is through the love which God shows in Christ. The hope which is experienced by people enduring hardship points to a God who collaborates with creation towards a hope which is, in part, realizable in this world. For Moltmann hope is grounded in the promises of God. He says that hope can be discerned in the liberating experiences of the Exodus, and the cross and resurrection of Jesus. In God's promises of faithfulness to a people, Hasler quotes Moltmann as saying, 'the hidden future already announces itself, and exerts influence in the present through the hope it awakens'.

Christian liberation and community work

I hesitate to write about Liberation Theology in this brief chapter, not only because the literature on the subject is considerable but also because Christian thinking has not been able to describe Liberation Theology in a British or European context. On the other hand, if anything is to be said about Liberation Theology in the West it is likely to come from the reflective experience of practitioners in community work. They form an alliance with others, like black Christians and some in the feminist theology movement, each of whom have experienced a struggle for recognition in a society with other priorities.

Liberation Theology has its origins in struggles for freedom in South America. Both the books of the Bible and the writings of Karl Marx are seen as providing a way of understanding the paradoxes and contradictions in society. It is an analysis of the contradictions which leads to a conflictual understanding of the way in which inequalities in society can be resolved. History, as well as being inherited, is made by those who are willing to use their various kinds of power to bring about social change. Black and feminist theologians say, however, that history has been written in ways that ignore the experience of their people or gender. Community workers and projects quite definitely exist at the interface of those with great social needs and those with the power to bring change – or to make matters worse.

Community workers would be wise not to commit themselves to one method only of working. Liberation Theology is vital in analysing power and in recognizing the place of the voiceless. But in order to bring about 'liberation' or social change, a range of methods may be used. In its modern, liberal, dress Christianity has become committed to tolerance, dialogue and reconciliation. These strands are as important for community work as is change through conflict or confrontation. It is a worry that broad-based organizing, rather than bringing wide-ranging change, is using the confrontational methods of social division to bring about rapid but localized social improvement. Christians involved in community work will bring Liberation Theology and its critiques into their method of critical reflection. However, they may decide on different paths of action according to their situations and long-term strategic aims.

Churches as agents for change?

There remains one difficult organizational question to be asked in this section about community work and the Christian faith. It is whether Churches, either as local congregations or as denominations, can be formative in bringing about social change. Doreen Finneran in *Faith in Community Development*, published in 1993, is both stimulating and pessimistic in her answers to this question.

She concluded that where local churches have done 'successful' pieces of community work it was as a result of their moving outside the mainstream structures and of collaborating with others. Finneran argues that the principal denominations, while describing themselves as agents of change, actually have a primary task of maintaining their own existence and of passing on tradition. Such a strong agenda will preclude radical, internal, structural change of the kind which is implied in the community development method.

Another difficulty which denominations have, according to Finneran, is the conflict between community development methods and the traditional leadership roles ascribed to the clergy. She says that both clergy and lay people find it difficult to work in a participative way, particularly in a church setting. The clergy are seen as part of an authoritarian, hierarchical structure and collude with expected ways of behaviour. Similarly, the clerically focused nature of the churches means that lay leadership is not recognized in a significant way.

Finneran reached these conclusions after a thorough survey of church-related community projects in the Manchester area. Some projects were significant in their own right and demonstrated considerable co-operation with secular agencies; but others in relation to the churches, as organizations with different agendas, continued to reject these methods of working within their own structures. She concludes with a depressing sentence about her survey: 'The developments used as case studies continue at a diocesan level to be ascribed solely to the work of idiosyncratic clergy.' Many who are committed to the promotion of community development methods within the denominations will say 'Amen' to that!

CASE STUDY
A voyage of discovery

I am a woman deacon in charge of an inner-city church with a well-established community project. The buildings are modern and multi-purpose. I have been in my present post for eleven years and shall stay until I retire in three years' time. Our present community worker, Diane, is about to leave when our Church Urban Fund grant comes to an end. The next appointment will be of a lay worker, funded by the Diocese.

Diane is not a church-goer and her absence on Sundays, except on special occasions, has distanced her from the congregation. Grievances have built up over her time here, though she is a professional and experienced community development worker.

In particular, Diane has taken over the small, young people's group called 'Discoverers' and has turned it into a large, open, junior youth group with an average of over fifty attenders and a parents' 'Management' Group. Church members have been invited to help but have stayed away. The Management Group have their own funds which they refuse to see as part of the church accounts. In addition, Diane has organized assertiveness training groups. Now, many of our volunteers can articulate their feelings of real ownership of the project and the premises.

In contrast the church members, who are mostly elderly, are inarticulate except in their own company, and at Church Council meetings. When Diane leaves they hope that, if unsupported, many of Diane's initiatives will fade away and that the new worker will organize more events 'for our own people and church'.

What could I have done to prevent the situation concerning Diane to deteriorate? What can I do to ensure the new worker 'gets off on the right foot' with both church and community?

Further Reading

The Parish Church, Giles Ecclestone (ed.) (Mowbray, 1988)
The Dynamics of Religion, Bruce Reid (Darton, Longman & Todd, 1978)

10

Evaluation and Stock-taking

Evaluating and taking stock of a project should not be a threatening or nerve-racking thing. For almost all of those who take part in an evaluation the experience will turn out to be something very good. Evaluation, or looking back in a guided way over your work, is a time when learning takes place, and gives a chance to review the events which have characterized life in a project. If the project has been a really significant piece of community work then very many people and groups will want to become involved, and will give freely of their time. Evaluation is only threatening to those who have something to hide. If that is the case, then a review of a piece of work is urgent and necessary.

Evaluation is not accusation, it is not a trial, it is not a way of bringing someone else in to get things out into the open that you should have taken responsibility for months ago. It is not a way of solving problems in a few hours which have taken months or years to create. Evaluation is a detailed look at the activities of your piece of work over a stated period of time, using methods which can come as close as possible to measuring effectiveness and change.

Evaluation does not award prizes or give out medals. It does not pronounce success or failure. It can help you to understand how you are doing and it can allow others to share in participating in your evaluation process.

Why evaluate a project?

For your own learning Life is often so busy that there is not time to think in a systematic way about what is going on in a piece of work. 'We coped with that crisis well' may be an adequate, immediate response but reflection or review might want to make you ask: 'Why do we continue to get crises? Who causes them – the people in the project or its structure and the way it is run?

What can be done to smooth out the panic-stricken, exhausting nature of our work?'

To compile an annual report Every publicly funded project is required to produce an annual report and to have properly presented and audited accounts. It is a great mistake to see these annual events as a chore which has to be completed before the 'real work' can be continued. Writing an annual report is a mini-evaluation. A studied look through the records and the writing about events over the past year can give a great sense of perspective and allow objectivity and learning to take place. In the same way, accounts tell a very real picture about the life of a project. Analysis of sources of income and types of expenditure can make facts leap from the page which were only hunches before. A budget is no more than crystal ball gazing if it is produced without an understanding of events and financial trends of the year before and without a realistic assessment of the needs for the year to come.

To secure funding Evaluation has to take place before grants can be applied for. Many major pieces of funding are for three years. If continuation funding is to be gained, or new money found, the whole of the life of a project will need to be examined by an outside person before major grant-making bodies will consider an application.

For the responsible employment of staff 'How am I doing?' is a frequent, unspoken request from staff in a community project. When everything seems fluid or is being done for the first time, and when there are no comparable projects to measure success by, then staff insecurity can arise. Many contracts will have a review date built into them. This is also a way to ensure that staff, supervisors and Management Committees can ask 'How are we doing?' Again, staff evaluation need not be a threatening exercise; it should aim at being a supportive, learning exercise for all concerned. Even if there is no money to continue to employ a member of staff, evaluation of the whole cycle of employment is very valuable. A well-written and researched piece of evaluation can help a member of staff to have another resource when they are looking for a new job.

Can you do it yourself?

Well, yes, but if you do decide to carry out an evaluation in this way you will have to ask yourselves 'Who is it for? Who will hope to gain by this method? Will it be the most effective way? Can we distance ourselves sufficiently from the work to be objective?', and a range of similar questions. A self-evaluation may be appropriate when:

- you are producing an annual report
- you are looking at one event in the life of your project
- you are examining particular internal incidents
- you want to learn from experience by conducting your own review
- you know that self-examination may be appropriate before a wider review takes place
- you feel staff and volunteers would welcome or need an opportunity to talk to one another about their work.

When is it best to get outside advice?

Those involved professionally will tell you almost always, of course. Given your internal needs as expressed in the list above, there will be times when you feel the need, or are compelled, to have an outside person to help you with a review.

An external person can be of benefit to the review process when they can:

- encourage staff to speak to an outsider, and to one another, in ways that they would not if they were alone
- bring an objectivity as an outsider, even when it is known that they have particular views and values about the ways in which community work is done
- bring professional skills to facilitate a wider process of consultation and discussion
- offer resources for writing up and producing an evaluation report
- encourage other groups to give time to comment on your project in a way that otherwise you could not
- frame and organize a review process in a way that no one in the project could do
- give a professionalism and credibility to your work which it needs at this stage in its development and which will be an asset in applying for further funding.

Budgeting for a review

Consultants are often expensive and you will need to anticipate the cost in your final year's budget. Churches live in a 'book token' culture and frequently hope to get professional work done without having to pay the full, or any, of the cost. There are agencies who can offer professional services at a reduced cost for voluntary organizations. Sometimes church employees on a denominational staff can be called upon to conduct an evaluation as part of their job.

Increasingly those with developed consultancy skills are moving out of employment by a church or voluntary organization, or even local authority, to become self-employed. It is in this reservoir of people that the most refined skills will often be found. They will need to charge fees and will always discuss them with you before they begin a piece of work. The Management Committee or Trustees of a project will have to decide on the scale of an evaluation. Here, as in much of the rest of life, you will get what you can pay for – and often what you deserve.

The professional skills involved in an evaluation will help you learn and grow. A piece of evaluation done badly can leave a very great deal of hurt, unhappiness and bitterness. It is certainly best to look at several people and types of evaluation before you decide what method you will undertake and who you will use.

What is being evaluated?

The project On the surface, and correctly, it is the actual piece of work which has been funded, and which began with aims and objectives, that is being reviewed after a stated period of time and for particular reasons.

The project and the churches In a wider sphere evaluation will explore the support, commitment and responsibility which sponsoring churches have continued to give. It may well look at what growth has taken place in their relationships with one another as a result of their commitment to this piece of work. A practical evaluation may provoke a parallel theological review, or audit, of the learning and change which has taken place within the churches.

The project and the community Evaluation will look at all the original partners in a project and how their commitment has varied. It will look at the project's aims in terms of collaborative community building and will try to gain some measure of the effectiveness of the community development which has taken place.

Project workers Those employed in a project may feel themselves particularly under scrutiny during an evaluation, and in a very real sense they are. A primary way to relieve tension and anxiety is to involve them in the planning of the process from the outset and to agree boundaries and their roles within the evaluation process. Good progress in the different stages of the evaluation is vital. Unfortunately it is common for a worker not to be told that there is dissatisfaction with them until there is a major blow-up or they are asked to leave. It is important that there is honesty about how the worker and employers feel about the work, and regular reviews can help to ensure that there is a proper opportunity to raise matters that may be avoided at a regular staff meeting. A possible format for a review/appraisal is given below:

Questions the job-holder should answer

Looking at your job description, say in which key tasks you have done well during the past year – give examples.

Which key tasks in your job description have not gone well? – give examples.

Are there any inappropriate key tasks in your job description? Have any been omitted? If so, please specify them.

How would you describe your overall performance in the last year? Summarize in one or two sentences.

List targets relating to your key tasks that you intend to achieve in the next year. A target is a measurable objective which can be achieved in a specific time.

List what you see to be your specific training and/or experience needs during the coming year.

Describe any particular help or support you feel you need in achieving your targets.

The Management Group It is sometimes difficult for those who have volunteered, or been pressed into, membership of a Management Group to understand why they should be subjected to an external review. If they have been properly briefed and have understood their task from the beginning, this should not be a problem. It is the responsibility of the Management Group and the Trustees to initiate a review. The real difficulties arise when they realize they are a part of it! Ultimate responsibility for a project and decisions about its future, or otherwise, rests with the Trustees.

The participants in a project Any evaluation of a piece of community work which did not include the active involvement of those for whom the project is intended would be fundamentally flawed.

This is much more than 'consumer research', it is the acid test of whether a really collaborative piece of work has been undertaken and whether any sense of partnership exists.

The components of evaluation

In *Measuring Success* by Rodney Hedley a clear and friendly method of getting into an assessment is described. To evaluate an activity it is necessary to consider the process involved in carrying it out. Suppose we went to a pensioners' social club and asked one of the participants a few questions about it. We might find the following:

Q: How did the social club start?

A: About two years ago one of the pensioners on the estate, Irene, said she was fed up sitting at home bored all day, with nothing to do but watch television. She reckoned there must be others like her. She looked around to see if there were any social activities for pensioners but found the only thing available was a lunch club. She found that wasn't very good: it was only open twice a week, was held a good distance from where most of the pensioners she knew lived, and was only open for an hour. She thought it would be a good idea to get some sort of social club going, and she was sure she would find support from other pensioners.

She knocked on doors and made a point of meeting other pensioners at places they usually went, like the post office, and she found they were very keen on the idea as they were just like her – a bit bored and lonely. They all thought the idea of a social club was a good one. Irene then went to the council and found that there was a disused room available. Very soon they opened up the room, got people going along, and since then the club has been open two afternoons a week.

Q: What goes on at the club?

A: Tea and biscuits are served. we have a bingo session. It's mostly chat. We have a radio. Jim, one of the pensioners, brings that in.

Q: Have you tried anything else?

A: Yes, it makes me laugh to think about it – someone tried to get us dancing! It was a flop. The women were interested but the men . . . Recently a few people have thought that we should have regular coach outings. Irene's investigating that.

Q: How is the club run?

A: Well I suppose you'd say we all run the club. We all help out. There is a sort of committee which meets once a month and we're all invited to it, but most of us don't bother, we're happy to leave it to Irene.

Q: What do people think of the club?

A: We've got more people coming now than when we started so I think that's a good sign. I mean, they wouldn't come if they didn't like it, would they? What's more, I think it's brought pensioners on the estate together. People are actually visiting each other in their own homes.

Q: So you don't think pensioners are as lonely or bored as they used to be?

A: No way.

It seems from the above description that this is a successful club. Can evaluation help us understand its success? We can refer to what researchers call the 'components of evaluation' which make up the process:

- the aims of the project
- the means used in the project
- the outcome of the project.

The *needs* expressed in this case were that there was a bored pensioner and 'she reckoned that there must be others like her'. She found them as well. But she also checked out the *resources*. She knew there was some sort of social activity – the lunch club – but that was inappropriate to the needs and difficult to get to. She also found a resource – the room.

The needs and resources were then transformed into an *aim*, to provide a social club for the estate, and then translated into action. The room, the tea, the biscuits, the bingo and the arrangements made by Irene were all part of the *means*. Then the *outcome*: not only good attendances but the person we spoke to seemed to think that pensioners on the estate were more friendly. So perhaps we might say that the original need of boredom and isolation was really being met.

All very obvious, one might say, but we shall probe deeper into the components. To begin with, the components are interlinked and form a cycle. So, for example, when the social club was formed it still remained responsive to need: tea dancing turned out to be a flop; coach outings seemed a better bet. Evaluation then has to recognize the continuous nature of the activity. We would have:

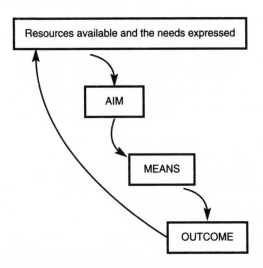

An evaluation exercise would seek to establish why the tea dancing flopped. Was it because the pensioners had no need of dancing? Or was it because their dancing need was met elsewhere – at the Darby and Joan Club which had opened shortly after Irene had started the club? Or was it because the men were so chauvinist? Or was the music awful?

More importantly, was the club really meeting the aim of providing a social club for the estate? Irene may have set out to do that but perhaps in setting up the club all she did was bring in her own social circle. Carrying out an evaluative exercise on the people who attended the club – finding out where they come from and how they got to know about the club – might give clues to whether the club really was for the estate, or for Irene. If a survey of people showed that the club was really a vehicle for Irene's friends, the decision might be to change the aim of the club to be more appropriate: call it 'Irene's Club'. Or it might be to change the means to ensure pensioners from all parts of the estate got involved.

In the following sections we will consider the components of evaluation more fully. But before we start, a useful exercise to try out for yourself is to state what you think the needs, resources, aims, means and outcomes of your own organization or project are. The questions, and space to answer, are in the box below. After you have completed the box consider:

1. Would people in your organization – Committee members, managers, paid staff, volunteers or clients – give very different answers?
2. All the questions in the box begin with 'What?'. Start to think about the 'How' of assessing the components.

Exercise on the components of evaluation

Answer very briefly

What are the needs your project/agency intends to meet?

_____

_____

What are the resources your project/agency has at its disposal?

_____

_____

What is the aim of your project/agency?

_____

_____

What 'means' does your project/agency use?

_____

_____

What is the outcome?

_____

_____

Key stages in the evaluation process

There are a number of key stages to be gone through in order that an effective review of a piece of work can take place. Some of these are essential and will be looked for by outside bodies, others are a matter of internal policy to be decided by individual groups.

Go back to your original aims Open up that long-forgotten file, buried in the cabinet or in a box somewhere, and look again at what you said your aims would be in setting up the project. Take each of them individually and look at where you are now, how you feel about the journey in between, and the differences which have emerged. Try to understand how you have evolved in a certain way and why. Look also at the values expressed in your aims and see if they have been maintained and still inform and inspire your work.

Go back to the Trust Deed Make a formal check of what your objectives are if you are registered as a charity. Check that you are still operating within the requirements of the law and that you have sent all the necessary sets of reports and accounts to the Charity Commissioners.

Draw a timeline Take a long sheet of newsprint or the back of a roll of wallpaper and fix it to the wall. Draw a line along the bottom with divisions for months or years. Then get everyone on the Management Committee, or as many of those involved in the review procedure as you can, to 'brainstorm' significant events in the life of the project.

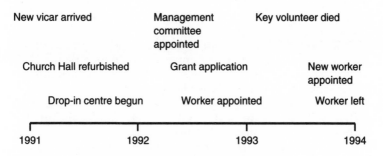

Look at the most significant events, the good times and the crises, and decide how to bring them into the review process.

Review underlying principles Whatever your original aims were it is likely that you will have learned much more about community work and community development through the experience of being actively involved. You may want to use a check-list of commonly held values in community work to look again at yourself and at the piece of work.

To be an effective community worker there are a number of concepts with which the worker must be familiar. In addition, they must have experience of work in a number of areas and share certain values. Sometimes these are listed under a heading of 'core competencies'.

As stated in Chapter 2, the Federation of Community Work Training Groups has adopted its Definition of Community Work as the starting point. The definition refers to the underlying values of community work. These values recognize a set of principles, which I have called the Ten Commandments of Community Work:

1. Respect of human rights
2. Vision of a society which is truly a participatory democracy, and where people contribute and receive as equals
3. Recognition that collaborative and collective working within our democracy is not always by equals, and that there are inequalities within communities which are severely damaged
4. Belief in the ability of all people to work positively together to change inequality
5. That community work must involve a process of action and reflection which moves towards clear goals, set collectively and evaluated continually
6. That such a process must also enable the empowerment of those with the least power, so that they can participate as equals
7. That groups must be self-determining, with those experiencing the problem in control of the outcomes
8. That individuals take responsibility for themselves and their own actions, and then recognize the influence their values have on other people. These values must constantly be appraised in the light of new learning
9. Giving support to individuals, groups and communities so that they can deal with conflict, and can challenge for themselves inequality and injustice
10. Appreciation of each other and the reality of each other's experience, and confirming and validating this as part of a process for real change within society.

You may also want to conduct a review of the use of individuals in relation to the project. This means:

• knowing their own strengths and weaknesses, and an ability to draw out others' strengths and weaknesses
• knowing their own values and an awareness of their effect on others

- an ability to organize themselves and set priorities, and be able to share these co-operatively
- they can develop ways of making themselves accountable
- they can find and use their own support structure
- welcoming positive and challenging supervision as a process of accountability and development
- having an awareness of the need to reappraise values and to extend their own learning
- knowing when they are not the appropriate person to be working with the group.

A review of how your group or committee has worked might include a look at how you have been functioning. This means:

- being able to negotiate a contract, both formally and informally; explaining their role, their lines of accountability and their involvement with the group
- enabling any group to set clear aims, and objectives and targets for the group's achievement
- assisting groups to develop appropriate ways of organizing, and being aware of the differences which race, class and gender bring to organizing
- assisting group members to develop specific group work skills, e.g. Chair, Secretary, Treasurer, Fund-raiser, Publicity person, etc. necessary for the maintenance of the group
- an awareness of the preparation required to set up a successful group
- when setting up groups, ensuring that there is equal access for membership, participation, etc.
- knowing how to maintain and withdraw from a group, and how to assist a group in closing its activity
- being aware of the way in which a group leader functions in order to enable participation and prevent domination
- an awareness of conflict within a group and finding different ways of bringing this out and resolving difficulties
- being aware of how to enhance the group's reflection on action, and how to involve everyone in a participatory way.

Conduct a Christian or theological review Do not be frightened by this suggestion. If the work has any Christian basis, or if Christians are involved in it, then there should be no surprise in the suggestion that God also might be discovered in the activities. One simple way of reflecting on the experience of God in a piece of work is to repeat the timeline exercise in a different way. Instead of the timescale being at the bottom of the page, draw it in the centre or two-thirds of the way down. In the bottom section write times when God has felt particularly present, or absent, or when you have wanted particular help:

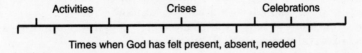

In doing this piece of reflection you will both be thinking about God in the way in which you have been working, and also making some connection, or observing the lack of them, between faith and actual events and times in your work.

Review values in your work This may be a different way of conducting a Christian review or it can be a way of examining your own personal values and ideals in relation to your work. It is also a useful method of connecting short-term activities, medium-term goals and your own system of values.

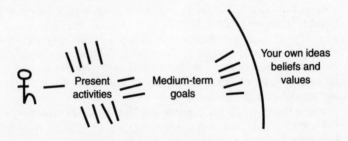

This is an important exercise because it not only makes a connection between activities, goals and values, but it makes you explore your own values and discuss them with others.

The fundamental question to be explored within this task is the relationship between your values and the other two areas. If there is a connection, or even a harmony, then it is likely that you are happy with your work and the level of job satisfaction is high. If there is a serious gap between what you do every day and your own beliefs and values, then it is likely that you will feel unhappy or frustrated in your work.

If this dissonance is a significant factor for you then a range of options present themselves. There needs to be an openness in discussion to see if others feel the same. If differences in values do emerge, and there is dissatisfaction within the project, then it might be appropriate to look at where the places are which signify differences. Is it between the workers and the Management Committee? Or is there a significant difference between the project and the sponsoring church or churches?

It is often the case that an openness about these differences at the time of an evaluation can be a learning and a healing thing. People who thought they were far apart begin to grow more closely together by discussing their differences in a way that has not been possible within the business-oriented, practical nature of day-to-day discussions.

There is, of course, the serious possibility that a worker, or a Committee member, a Trustee or a member of a church does find that their values are different from those of other people. If a project is seen in a significantly different way, or if a job is interpreted differently, there is always the real and honest option for people to part company and go to work, or to a group or church, where they can share their values more happily with others. Openness in discussion can make an agreement to differ and go a different way a mutually understood decision. This way of conducting discussion can help misunderstandings to be brought out into the open and prevent people, projects and even churches feeling let down, betrayed or just plain confused. Other sections of this book dealing with conflict and resolving differences may be helpful in connection with such a review.

Conduct a community development review For such a review it will be helpful to refer to the range of descriptions of community care, community work, etc. in Chapter 2. A basic understanding of what kind of work you are undertaking has to underpin the nature of any evaluation.

The recommendations

When the process of evaluation is complete there is likely to be a report produced, or even a series of reports if there have been a range of levels at which the review has been conducted. Different people will need to take responsibility for different aspects of the recommendations in the review. The worst possible outcome is for recommendations to be ignored, not accepted, and the report shelved. Avoiding the truth about your work as others see it could be the next step towards the death of a project. It will very likely mean continued unhappiness within the project and make successful applications for further grants even more unlikely.

There are very simple guidelines which will help with the examination and implementation of recommendations following a review:

- What is the recommendation?
- How can it be acted upon?
- Who should take action?
- What resources will they need?
- By when will action need to be completed?
- Who will monitor it?

In conclusion, it needs to be emphasized that the process of evaluation will be a positive experience if as many people as possible can become involved. Much of the change needed in a project will be started through the process of discussion. Often the final report will summarize conclusions in which there is general agreement and where action has already begun.

If there are difficulties then it is even more important to use an outside consultant. It may be a greater help to use a new person or group to help with the next stage of your work. Remember, the health of a project, like the health of a nation or a community, can be measured by the way in which differences can be tolerated and by the ways in which people with different skills and abilities can learn to live and work together in harmony.

Further Reading

Measuring Success, Rodney Hedley (Neighbourhood Care Action Programme/Advance, 1985)

Useful Organizations and Addresses

In telephone numbers the code or number in brackets may be used until 16 April 1995, when it is replaced by the preceding code or number.

Adult Network
Adult Education Dept.
Board of Education
Church House
Great Smith Street
London SW1P 3NZ
0171 (071)-222 9011

Advisory, Conciliation and Arbitration Service
27 Wilton Street
London SW1X 7AZ
0171 (071)-210 3000

Association of Community Workers
Stevenson Building
Elswick Road
Newcastle upon Tyne NE4 6SQ

Catholic Bishops' Conference Committee for Community Relations
39 Ecclestone Square
London SW1V 1PP
0171 (071)-834 8692

Central Council for Education and Training In Social Work
26 Park Row
Leeds LS1

Church Action on Poverty
Central Buildings
Oldham Street
Manchester M1 1JT
0161 (061)-236 9321

Church Urban Fund
2 Great Peter Street
London SW1P 3LX
0171 (071)-222 7010
Fax: 0171 (071)-799 1829

Churches Community Work Alliance
82 Swan Gardens
Erdington
Birmingham B23 6QG
0121 (021)-384 8744 (also fax)

**Commission for Racial
Equality**
Elliot House
10–12 Allington Street
London SW1E 5EH
0171 (071)-828 7022

**Community and Youth Work
Union**
Unit 202a
The Ardent Centre
60 Frederick Street
Birmingham B1 3HS
0121 (021)-233 2815

Employment Service
Rockingham House
123 West Street
Sheffield S1 4ER

**Equal Opportunities
Commission**
Overseas House
Quay Street
Manchester M3 3HN
0161 (061)-833 9244

**Evangelical Urban Training
Project**
c/o 127 City Road
Sheffield S2
0114-275 6856 (0742-756856)

**Federation of Community
Work Training**
356 Glossop Road
Sheffield S10 2NL
0114-273 9391 (0742-739391)

**Federation of Independent
Advice Centres**
Concourse House
Lime Street
Liverpool L1 1NY
0151 (051)-709 7444

Frontier Youth Trust
Scripture Union
130 City Road
London EC1V 2NJ

**Lesbian and Gay
Employment Rights**
St Margaret's House
21 Old Ford Road
London E2 9PL

**London Voluntary Service
Council**
356 Holloway Road
London N7 6PA
0171 (071)-700 8107
Fax: 0171 (071)-700 8108

**Mission Alongside the Poor
Programme**
Methodist Church Home
Missions Division
1 Central Buildings
Westminster
London SW1H 9NN
0171 (071)-222 8010
Fax: 0171 (071)-233 0323

NACRO
169 Clapham Road
London SW9 0PU

**National Council of
Voluntary Organizations**
26 Bedford Square
London WC1B 3HJ

New Ways to Work
309 Upper Street
London N1 2TY
0171 (071)-226 4026

Relate National
Herbert Gray College
Little Church Street
Rugby CV21 3AP
01788 (0788)-573241

Salford Urban Mission
49 Acresfield Road
Salford M6 7GE

**Standing Conference for
Community Development**
356 Glossop Road
Sheffield S10 2NL
0114-270 1718 (0742-701718)

**United Reformed Church
Community Ministry Dept.**
86 Tavistock Place
London WC1H 9RT
0171 (071)-837 7661
Fax: 0171 (071)-833 9262

Urban Theology Unit
210 Abbeyfield Road
Sheffield S4 7AZ
0114-243 5342 (0742-435342)

Voice of the People Trust
277 Reddings Lane
Tyseley
Birmingham B11 3DD

Westhill College
Weoley Park Road
Birmingham B29 6LL
0121 (021)-414 0104

William Temple Foundation
Manchester Business School
Manchester M15 6PB
0161 (061)-275 6533

YMCA National College
640 Forest Road
London E17 3DZ
0181 (081)-530 5599

Bibliography

Sandy Adirondack, *Just About Managing* (LVSC, 1992).

Saul D. Alinsky, *Reveille for Radicals* (Vintage Books, 1969) and *Rules for Radicals* (Vintage Books, 1972).

Archbishop's Commission, *Faith in the City* (Church House Publishing, 1985) and *Faith in the Countryside* (Church House Publishing, 1990).

T. R. Batten, *The Non-Directive Approach in Group and Community Work* (OUP, 1967).

Board for Social Responsibility of the Church of England, *Church and Community Work* (Church House Publishing, 1987).

Yvonne Craig, *Learning for Life: A handbook of adult religious education* (Mowbray, 1994).

Philip and Jonathan Evans, *Despair and Hope in the City* (Voice of the People Trust, 1990).

Federation of Community Work Training Groups, 'Definition of community work', *Bulletin* (January 1989).

Doreen Finneran, *Faith in Community Development* (University of Manchester, 1993).

Forbes, Hayle and Reason, *Voluntary But Not Amateur* (LVSC, 1992).

Laurie Green, *God in the Inner City* (Urban Theology Unit, 1993) and *Power to the Powerless* (Marshall Pickering, 1987).

Joseph Hasler, *Becoming Human Together* (Diocese of Bristol, 1992).

A. Hawley and P. Bradley, *The Church and Urban Communities* (University of Liverpool, 1988).

Rodney Hedley, *Measuring Success* (Neighbourhood Care Action Programme/Advance, 1985) and *Neighbourhood Care in Practice* (LVSC, 1984).

Inner-City Religious Council, *Faith in Inner Cities* (1993).

George Lovell, *The Church and Community Development* (Grail, 1972).

Jay McLeod, *Community Organizing: A practical and theological appraisal* (Christian Action, 1994).

M. Parker, *Leading Groups* (Methodist Church Division of Ministries, 1987).

James Pitt and Maurice Keane, *Community Organizing? You've never really tried it?* (Birmingham: J. & P. Consultancy, 1984).

L. St Louis and J. Ashdown, *Outline of Basic Skills in Community Work Course* (1993).

Alan Stanton, *Invitation to Self-Management* (Dab Hand Press, 1989).

Urban Theology Unit, *A Petition of Distress from the Cities* (1993).

Catherine Widdicombe, *Group Meetings That Work* (St Paul Press, 1994).

William Temple Foundation, *Community Work in the New Context* (1989), *The New Worker* (1991) and *The New Boss* (1993).

Your Neighbourhood Group (Neighbourhood Care Action Programme, 1985).